THE QUIET IMPERATIVE

THE QUIET IMPERATIVE

Meditations on Justice and Peace

Based on Readings from the New Testament

JOHN CARMODY

THE UPPER ROOM
Nashville, Tennessee

Scripture quotations not otherwise identified are from the Revised Standard
Version of the Bible, copyrighted 1946, 1952, and © 1971 by the Division
of Christian Education, National Council of the Churches of Christ in the
United States of America, and are used by permission.

Scripture quotations designated NJB are excerpts from THE NEW JERUSA-
LEM BIBLE copyright © 1985 by Darton, Longman & Todd, Ltd. and
Doubleday & Company, Inc. Reprinted with permission of the publisher.

Scripture quotations designated TEV are from the *Good News Bible, the
Bible in Today's English Version,* copyrighted by American Bible Society
1966, 1971, © 1976, and are used by permission.

"International Sufferings" is adapted in part from "Way of the Cross in
the World" by the author, which first appeared in *Praying: Spirituality for
Everyday Living,* No. 6. *Praying* was a supplement to and published by the
National Catholic Reporter.

The lithograph, "Evening Village," that appears on the cover is by
Cynthia December.

Cover and Book Design: Roy Wallace
First Printing: October 1986 (5)
Library of Congress Catalogue Card Number: 86-50917
ISBN: 0-8358-0518-2

Printed in the United States of America

For LOU PETRILLO

CONTENTS

PREFACE

This book is, as the subtitle promises, a collection of meditations on peace and justice. The collection assumes Christian faith and it develops in three stages. First, the book deals with what I call "background" matters: reflections on the current state of affairs worldwide and on the connotations that "peace" and "justice" traditionally have carried in Christian circles. Second, it contains ruminations on some texts from the New Testament that try to cast light on peace and justice by working with the rich texture of this portion of scriptural revelation. Third, it turns more resolutely to practice, offering meditations on some of the attitudes we must have if we are to become makers of peace and doers of justice. In this third section I also reflect on some of the principal obstacles to proper Christian praxis.

At the end of the book stands an annotated bibliography in which the diligent reader will find not only fuller information about some of the books mentioned in the running text but also further leads for study. The list hardly is exhaustive, as peace and justice could center a wonderfully full library, but if one were interested in tracking down the sources of these sources, one would get deep into the bowels of such a library.

At the end of each chapter stands a triad of questions for reflection and discussion. Perhaps I should say clearly that I mean these questions to be provocative rather than informational.

Many of them have no simple answer, but thinking hard about nearly any of them should make "peace" and "justice" richer and more demanding notions.

My thanks to Charla Honea and the staff of the Upper Room for proposing and expediting this project; to my wife Denise for her customary support, patience, and irreverence; and to Lou Petrillo, who popped from the crowd of people who have demonstrated for me what a hunger for peace and justice might look like and have raised up warm feelings of dedication.

I

BACKGROUND
MEDITATIONS

1

International Sufferings

Read Matthew 5:1–16

In 1976 I made a trip around the world. For six months my work was to absorb what I could of foreign cultures. As I think back, this task entailed many confrontations with sufferings I had seldom seen in middle-class American neighborhoods.

In Europe, gypsies stationed themselves outside many churches. I never knew how honest their begging was, but each tug at my sleeve reminded me they have long been Europe's despised wanderers. In Cairo, little children, hitching rides on the back of buses, had no place to play but in the dangerous streets. In Jerusalem, Israeli soldiers patrolled outside the famous mosques. In India, lepers peered in the windows of country buses, and street vendors slept the night on pushcarts.

I saw nothing of outright famine, no actual riots or war. My trip bypassed East Africa and Southeast Asia. But in Greece, Iran, India, and Thailand, I saw enough disadvantaged and dispossessed people to last a lifetime.

Perhaps two-thirds of the world's more than five billion people live well below what we in the United States call the poverty line. Some population experts have predicted that by the year 2100 the world could have twenty billion people. (In the late 1970s there was a net gain of about 150,000 people a day; about 350,000 births and 200,000 deaths.)

By the year 2000 half the world's population likely will be living in cities, more than half such people unable to find jobs. Mexico City could swell to 31 million, Tokyo to 24 million, Shanghai to 23 million, Sao Paulo and New York to 21 million. Even if population growth slows and these predictions don't come true, children born in 1985 will inhabit a world at least five times as densely populated as that of their great-grandparents, with all the attendant pressures.

In 1900 world population was about 1.6 billion. What will the back streets of Hong Kong, already teeming, look like in 2050? Where will the traffic of New Delhi go? Already the abortion rate in Japan outstrips the rate of births. What problems does today's travail not force us to anticipate?

Despite their necessity, population figures and possible future scenarios are less moving than individual stories. I think of coming out of a hotel in Bangkok at mid-morning and bumping into a drunken Westerner with a Thai prostitute. The girl looked about thirteen, and already her life was badly twisted. A friend of mine works in Honduras, teaching in a boys' trade school. He admires his students' strength and resiliency. In nearby Nicaragua and El Salvador, such boys carry rifles. Their mothers can only protest futilely when they disappear.

The impression one gets from books is equally distressing. For instance, the books of V. S. Naipaul on India and the modern Muslim countries, like the novels of Alan Paton about South Africa, tell more of suffering and spiritual disease than of healthy, happy households. Yes, God does give all people sufficient grace for salvation. Yes, even very poor people often still dance and sing. But the people in our world not lashed by hunger or political oppression, free to raise healthy children and see their talents expand, are a pitifully small minority.

If God wants all human beings to flourish (Saint Irenaeus said that God's glory is human beings fully alive), God must be deeply saddened by our use of the world's resources. Almost everywhere there are enough resources for a modest population to live simply and well. Almost everywhere, though, human deficiencies force the majority to worry and suffer.

We have to believe that God's spirit is present to all worriers and sufferers. Our faith in a good God forces such an obligation upon us. Yet we know from both faith and common sense that God has given the world into our hands.

As Genesis 1:28 puts it, we are to increase, multiply, fill the earth, and subdue it. The disorders of the world, the sufferings far and wide, directly concern us. Especially in the realm of human relations—the worldwide economy, military stances, politics, and the like—things out of joint are things for which God holds us accountable. As the servant who hid his talents received the master's rebuke, so we must expect God to rebuke our having let so much land become waste, so many brothers and sisters starve.

Many of the sufferings one sees outside the United States stem from the nations' preparations for war. When even very poor countries pour large parts of their resources into weapons, the trade in arms has become a direct cause of starving children. The world over, military budgets waste money that should be going for education, health care, and higher culture. It is not an accident that preparations for war and huge national debts now coincide. Millions of people suffer because their countries cannot have both guns and butter, both ugly arms and beautiful homes.

I remember talking with Phillip Berryman and Stanley Rother, both of whom had served many years as missionaries in Guatemala. I asked them about the leaders of the regime there. Berryman smiled grimly and said perhaps the only analogy an American might understand would be the Mafia. Get in the way of the Mafia and you can expect to be wiped out. Get in the way of the powerholders in Guatemala and you will find yourself on a death-list.

Stanley Rother agreed, telling quietly of his work with an obscure Indian tribe far from the center of Guatemalan politics. He had only returned to the United States, in fact, because he had been warned by friends that his name was on the death-lists. And just what had been his crime? By ministering to the Indians, who are the poorest of Guatemala's poor, had he cast a spotlight on injustices the government wanted kept hidden?

Several months after this conversation I opened *Time* magazine and found myself staring at Stanley Rother's picture. He had gone back to his beloved Indians in the bush, and *Time* was reporting his murder. He was the first American missionary killed in Guatemala. His story remains for me a summary of international sufferings.

The Indians of Guatemala, like the Indians and blacks of the United States, gather together the worst strands of the sufferings that afflict so many. Although they have lived on the land for tens of thousands of years, they are the closest to their society's margins. In the eyes of the powerholders and the wealthy, they exist only to provide brute labor. Through the 1970s, the share of the economy possessed by Latin America's poor actually decreased, while the share of the wealthy rose.

When a Latin American country such as Nicaragua goes through revolution, poor people like the native Indians often become pawns in a bloody game. Again and again reports tell of their men being slaughtered at the soldiers' whim, of their women being raped. It seems a bestial violence races through the land, and they can only try to hide behind their insignificance. The personal implications I see for us North Americans are sharper than I'd like. Our dollars support the Latin American dictatorships. Our influence props the landowners. In too many places, children suffer and good people are murdered with what I can only assume to be our leaders' tacit permission. Do we really believe a just God will not ask us for an accounting?

How responsible are human beings for human starvation?
Why do even poor nations spend hundreds of millions of dollars for military arms?
What are the main emotions Christ probably feels toward those who suffer in our world?

2

Sufferings in the United States

Read Matthew 6:19–34

"The Talk of the Town" in *The New Yorker* of August 19, 1985, contained a quite remarkable little reflection. The anonymous writer described attending a concert at the Museum of Modern Art and being offended by the behavior of the crowd of people who had arrived too late to gain admission to the limited number of seats. Irritated that they could not get in, the crowd chanted "Let us in!" in an effort to disrupt the concert. The author returned to his condominium in New York after the concert and found a leaflet urging him to complain to the police about the vagrants, loiterers, and panhandlers regularly milling around the building. The juxtaposition of the two incidents—the petulant crowd outside the museum and the nose-in-air crowd of condominium owners—brought home the nastiness that both have-nots and haves can exhibit. To the author's mind, apathy in the face of the sufferings of other Americans would be bad enough. Hostility toward such powerless people as the derelict street-people is worse, since it warps our very humanity:

> Apathy is sad. Hostility toward the powerless is warping. Our lives and our frailties may not allow us to do what is right (though the example of saints and heroes—the fact that it *can* humanly be done—is always disturbing). We walk by people; that is more convenient than helping them. But when we raise our convenience up as an idol—when we insist that we can't stand even to *see* vagrants, loiterers, and panhandlers—we make an asser-

17

tion of our right to be comfortable which is as militant, as radical, as Mother Teresa's assertion of her duty to administer comfort.

I find this statement powerful in itself, but all the more significant because it appears in the pages of *The New Yorker*. *The New Yorker* advertises opulence and the good life. Yet life in New York so clearly denies riches, and even minimal amenities, to so many thousands that writers for the *The New Yorker* have to cope with the sufferings of the poor. To this author's credit, the sufferings of the poor are linked with the attitudes of the more fortunate. He or she realizes that all New Yorkers share a habitat or niche and interact. The taxes levied on the wealthy support the shelters (horrible places, according to the author) that the street-people will only go to as a last resort.

The system that rewards certain kinds of cleverness and dependability while penalizing those who can't keep pace is almost bound to produce haves and have-nots. The sufferings that come from this system are not themselves wholly unfair. They become horribly unfair, terribly inhumane, when people try to canonize them as judgments of God or reasons for despising those who can't measure up. At the point where we can't bear the sight of bums and failures, Jesus becomes a blazing accuser. For unless we have lost all memory of the biblical Christ, we recall that Jesus consorted with the taxgatherers and prostitutes—the despised moral failures of his day.

Sufferings in the United States are not more grievous than sufferings abroad, but the supposedly Christian basis of our culture can make them more poignant. If millions of people have to live on our streets, their only heat in winter the hot air of building vents or sidewalk registers, while millions more live in superabundance, the equality of the people of God seems cruelly mocked. Suffering in the United States, we might say, is more obviously theological in its implications. Ultimately, of course, suffering is theological everywhere, because everywhere God grieves that human beings must live in pain. But in countries of Christian background such as the United States, the theological implications should be more obvious. We cannot claim to be a Christian nation if we are despising the poor and repenting little of the attitudes that relegate the poor to the margins of society where we may not have to notice them.

That, of course, is the religious side of the statistics on unemployment, welfare, drug abuse, malnutrition, illiteracy, toxic pollution, and the like. All of those statistics stem from policies that we as a people have generated or sanctioned or tolerated. It would be a useless exercise in guilt-mongering to propose that we each hold ourselves responsible for the deficiencies in our social systems. If the standard of a realistic system of social services were only what people tend to achieve worldwide, we Americans would not have to feel too bad. But the fact remains that our country brims with physical and emotional sufferings. The fact remains that economic injustices and domestic violence send many to sleep at night desolate. For every celebrity who suffers a frightening disease buoyed by national sympathy, a hundred victims of cancer and other diseases suffer obscurely. Among the citizenry of one of the world's most fortunate nations, suffering and sadness take no holiday.

Sometimes mental snapshots, like that of the teenage Thai prostitute seemingly caught on the outskirts of hell, linger for months to keep compassion lively. I remember being irritated one moving day by the visit of a shy woman and her fresh-faced, preteen daughter. We were in the midst of final cleaning, our barricades of boxes having finally fallen to the movers, when these two wandered in to chat. Our time being short, my first instinct was that this was an interruption we certainly didn't need. Then I realized who the couple were. My wife had stood by the woman in a messy child-custody case, and the woman had felt bound to come to say a final thanks. Naturally shy, and often reduced by her crisis to inarticulate tears, she had previously met Denise on campus or sent her daughter by with gifts from their garden. Now she had to take a last look at her counselor and friend, as though she wasn't sure she would be able to find a kindly face to replace her. Whatever our hassles from moving, they were nothing compared to the sense of loss and fragility the woman was suffering. When she left, I returned to my cleaning quite chastened. I had nearly missed the significance of the visit of an angel, a messenger from the holy God.

The poet T. S. Eliot spoke of having the experience and missing the meaning. This occurs in our country day after day. Federal officials, including the highest officers of the land, visit slums and areas devastated by hurricanes. They want to be seen attending to their people's worst ills. And no doubt they are often moved by the sufferings they witness. But the meaning of their experiences seldom comes through to them with anything like biblical clarity. If it did, they would not be able to continue with business as usual. If it did, they would be converted to a championing of the poor, like the championing that Jesus expressed in the Beatitudes. The poor have the kingdom of heaven, where they sit as the apple of God's eye, because the poor dramatize the difference between God's sense of justice and our sense. As the biblical prophets saw, God cares little for the properties of official ceremonies unless these sit atop a social structure driven by justice and mercy. Amos and Hosea, for instance, criticized biblical Israel because its widows and orphans meant less than the rectitude of its official cult. Sometimes our civil cult, the ceremonies in which our highest officials are the leading actors, seem designed to distract us from the items that should be at the top of the nation's agenda. Sometimes we seem to have all too few prophetic figures insisting that justice roll down like a mighty stream and all too many money-managers and rock stars.

The sufferings of people in the United States are no more important than the sufferings of people in Cambodia or Benin, yet certainly they are at least equally instructive. Most of the people in foreign countries live in a situation that makes no pretense of honoring ideals like those expressed in the Beatitudes. Most of our people who suffer neglect or are despised for taking up space on the sidewalk can claim the special status of the lost one that the Good Shepherd prefers to the ninety-nine that are safe.

What rights should panhandlers have?

How does AIDS focus the distinction between sinners and their sins?

What is an acceptable, truly realistic set of statistics on unemployment?

3

Christian Compassion

Read John 11:25–44

To reach the justice and peace implied in the gospel, we have to note the compassion that Jesus felt for all suffering people and try to imitate it. Whether the person who stood before him in pain was a fellow Jew or a foreigner, Jesus would be moved by the person's plight. The smallest expression of faith in God or in Jesus himself would move Jesus to intercede on the person's behalf. Insofar as Jesus represents for us the human face of God, we can conclude that God is moved to the quick by human suffering. As the prophets sometimes depict the Lord as moved like a mother affected by the sufferings of her child, so the evangelists depict Jesus as tenderhearted. Thus when Jesus saw Mary weeping because of the death of her brother Lazarus, "he was deeply moved in spirit and troubled" (John 11:33).

This tenderheartedness sometimes gets Christians a bad name. The tough-minded pragmatists are quick to label as "bleeding hearts" any who oppose their conviction that society runs by the law of the jungle. We can do little to deflect the core of this judgment, since the gospel compels us to believe that the law of the jungle has ceded to Christ's law of the cross. What we can deflect are the criticisms that come when we refuse to connect our tender hearts to balanced, realistic heads. The same Jesus who is compassionate toward the multitudes and weeps over Jerusalem holds few illusions about human weakness. As the opposition to his preaching of the kingdom of God rises, he realizes that he probably will have to die for his convictions. Similarly, as his disciples prove extremely slow to understand what sort of a Messiah he is, Jesus accepts their limitations. The Gospel of Mark, which most dramatizes the fact that Jesus was a suffering Messiah, never makes Jesus a fanatic or hopeless idealist. Sufficient for each day are the troubles that that day brings. God will provide for the morrow. And at some mysterious level, the morrow, like today, will ask us to accept the fact that God puts up with, is patient with, an imperfect, even an evil creation. Thus the compassion of Christ entails few illusions that good will or fine feelings alone will make the world bright and shining. The compassion of Christ asks us to identify ourselves with the way things are, the sufferings that are well-nigh unavoidable, while it also asks us to follow Christ's lead in removing the sufferings that we can.

Again and again we find both Jesus and the New Testament message remarkably balanced on this point. Jesus preaches that the time has arrived when things can be as they ought to be: just and peaceful. If people will repent and take this joyous message to heart, the blind can see and the poor be buoyed by good news. Yet Jesus is seldom surprised that many people fail to take his message to heart. Before long, the opposition of the Jewish leaders (who become Jesus' regular foes in the evangelists' story-telling) becomes just another part of Jesus' landscape, like the hills around Galilee. This is not to say that Jesus doesn't continue to be hurt when people reject him, nor that he doesn't continue to feel that such rejection marks them as closed. The compassion of Christ actually heightens his sense of justice and what ought to be so. But it is to say that a certain cool levelheadedness emerges in all the evangelists' portraits. Jesus knows what is in human beings' hearts and he never puts his deepest hopes in their hands. Always his deepest hopes repose in God.

What does this suggest for the compassion we might start to feel for street-people or mothers caught up in wrenching battles for custody of their children? First, that we let this emotion develop and not immediately write it off as wrongheaded or unrealistic. Not to be moved by human suffering is a sign that our spirits are barely alive. The more that other people's pain moves us to the quick and makes us identify with them helpfully, the more human, religious, and Christian we are.

The second implication is that we note how our first phase of emotional identification tends to run its course and then give way to a second phase of more sober reflection. In the first phase, we get beyond our initial repugnance at the dirt or drunkenness of the panhandler and give him a dollar. In the second phase, we think about what he probably will do with that dollar and then about ways of lessening the incidence of panhandling, alcoholism, destitution, and the like. The compassion ideally remains. We continue to let ourselves be troubled by the wretchedness of the man's bloodshot eyes and broken spirit. But we face rather soberly the strong hold his alcoholism no doubt has on him and the difficulty of rehabilitating the tens of thousands of people who have gotten themselves into situations like his.

I think that faith becomes especially necessary toward the end of this second, more reflective phase. For, ultimately, we face the temptation to think that we can do nothing for society's destitute people and so perhaps shouldn't waste time lamenting their fate or trying radically to change the current social structures that seem to hold them captive. Faith can move mountains, Jesus said, and at this point we need to move away mountains of reasons for despair. So we can call it an inspiration of faith when we tell ourselves that the man may use our dollar for a meal rather than a drink, or when we muse, probably more realistically, that even if our dollar goes for more drink, it might be an act of kindness that made the man's day less than fully bleak. And we can also call it an inspiration of faith when we think of finding out more about the dimensions of the problem of panhandlers, or more about the people who are trying to help them, or more about the political pressures that getting better shelters would entail. Best of all, when we actually are moved to do something to improve the panhandlers' situation—either something on the level of one-to-one charity or something on the level of welfare agencies and structures—we can say that faith is making our compassion effective.

Christian compassion has the tendency to become a stable angle of vision. In its grasp, we are more aware of just about every human being's vulnerability. So, for example, one starts to hear the fear behind the hard line being put forward by the oil baron who is lashing out at the regulators. The similar hard line put forward by the aged professor who is opposed to new, interdisciplinary studies strikes one as rather sad. Neither of these judgments should be the whole story. Both hard lines, if moved toward action, will have rippling effects that we have to calculate in terms of the overall common good. But it will cost us little and reward us greatly to linger a bit with the perception that even these apparently hard-boiled, almost frighteningly strong people may well be expressing deep-seated anxieties. If we let this perception clarify, we can identify with these people more sympathetically. That in turn can help us communicate to them that we somewhat understand their situation and find it reasonable. When we have reached that point, half our work of figuring out a compromise or trying to get them to see the other side of the story is accomplished.

One of the high points in the appreciation of compassion that we find in the New Testament occurs in Hebrews 5, where the discussion is of Jesus' priesthood. First the author stresses the human foundations of priesthood in general: "Every high priest is taken from among human beings and is appointed to act on their behalf in relationships with God, to offer gifts and sacrifices for sins; he can sympathize with those who are ignorant or who have gone astray, because he too is subject to the limitations of weakness" (5:1-2, NJB; this passage obviously should be understood as embracing the Christian ministry of women as well as men). Then the author makes a more acute application to Christ, focusing on the depth of vulnerability that Jesus showed in his passion and death: "In his life on earth, Jesus made his prayers and requests with loud cries and tears to God, who could save him from death. Because he was humble and devoted, God heard him" (5:7, TEV). The conclusion to this line of reflection, anticipated in Hebrews 4, is the famous lines: "Our High Priest is not one who cannot feel sympathy for our weaknesses. On the contrary, we have a High Priest who was tempted in every way that we are, but did not sin" (4:15, TEV). Christian compassion, therefore, is a circle running among ourselves, the fellow human beings to whom we reach out in sympathy, and the Christ whose vulnerable humanity gives us the confidence to believe that God is compassionate toward us. It is a blessed circle, supplying most of what we need to see the task of working for justice and peace realistically.

How does the passion of Christ figure in Christian compassion for other people?

What is the realism Christ shows toward human motivation?

Do the pros of giving a panhandler a dollar outweigh the cons?

4

The Quiet Imperative

Read 1 Corinthians 12:4–26

Compassion is such a central translation of Jesus' love of neighbor that it becomes an imperative voice sounding in Christians' consciences. Yet, like the voice that brought the presence of the Lord to the prophet Elijah (1 Kings 19:12), this voice is quiet and unpretentious. We are indeed called to hunger and thirst for justice and peace, but this calling itself is peaceful—something for the long haul. In our day, Christian ethicians have come to see that compassion means trying to rework the structures through which societies achieve (or fail to achieve) much of their justice and peace. This work stretches forth as a very long haul indeed, so the best way to approach it is quite matter-of-factly. When we have assumed that our faith will mean a lifelong effort to improve the lot of the suffering, we have begun to estimate correctly the centrality of peace and justice. When we have gained the further insight that a bedrock commitment to making our society more just and peaceful will place us on the outs with goodly numbers of our fellow citizens (and fellow churchgoers), we will have learned how and why all Christian faith must be prophetic.

Not very much in this learning process is dramatic. In itself a commitment to making one's society more just is as obvious as following the light of a good conscience. Take the example of the panhandlers and derelicts outside the building of condominiums. One has only to see the plight of these unfortunates to perceive that something is sadly amiss. It may take some time and effort to unravel the practical implications of this perception, but simple honesty will force one to consider the presence of the panhandlers a sign that something out of control is crying out for correction. If the first characterization of a healthy moral intelligence or conscience is a consistency between what one knows and what one does, then noting the situation around the condominiums becomes a pressure to vote, lobby, and generally shape one's citizenship so as to eliminate such snarls in the system.

The problem of derelicts, like the problem of messy divorces leading to traumatic fights about the custody of children, obviously consists of more than just snarls in the system. The structure of human society may incline some people toward dereliction, but a great deal of what even derelicts become is a matter of choices they have made. Similarly, nothing in even our sexually free culture determines that a marriage will turn bitter and break apart. We can get so immersed in statistics about unemployment and divorce that we forget the uniqueness of each situation. The imperative one feels to try to make society better cannot ride roughshod over other people's individuality and personal responsibility. That is another reason why it is a quiet, rather than a loud and bullying, imperative. Our job is to lessen the likelihood of dereliction and divorce, to improve the supports that people need if they are to work well and live in marital peace. By our example, our political activity, our charitable contributions, and our prayers, we have to try to build up the side of the angels. People may still choose the side of despair or Satan or selfishness, but we shall at least know that we have tried to offer them a more excellent way.

Consider, for instance, a little house church faced with a member who blows hot and cold. One year he is a regular member of the group, pulling his fair share of the burdens of both prayer and social service that the little community has taken on itself. The next year his marriage has fallen apart, he has taken up with another woman and dropped out of the group. The third year he wants to rejoin the group. His marriage remains in tatters, but he has dropped the harmful affair and is again groping for repentance and spiritual sustenance. Because of his erratic behavior, several members of the group wish he would stay away. Because of their overall sense that judgment belongs to God more than to themselves, the group as a whole decides to welcome him back. The man is not one who speaks about his situation or degree of recommitment forthrightly. The group has to decide how he is doing by how he behaves. He behaves ambiguously, still seeming to hanker for an exciting liaison yet sometimes coming back to a sterner self-discipline. Is the group correct in thinking that bearing with him patiently is wise?

I think the group is correct. As I read the quiet imperative to forward the work of justice and peace, groups such as this, like individual Christians, have to make what impact a situation seems to allow. Occasionally they may be called to such dramatic acts of witness as quitting their jobs in protest against the buildup of nuclear arms or reading the riot act to an erring member of their community. More often the task will be quietly demonstrating a more excellent way. In the case of concern about nuclear arms, the more excellent way might be supporting moratoria on the production of weapons and new agreements to control the spread of nuclear technology. In the case of the wishy-washy member of the home church, the more excellent way might be the witness to fidelity and the nonjudgmental support that continuing to make him feel welcome would express.

We seldom find ourselves in clear-cut situations where the way to honor our call to justice and peace is obvious. Usually there are things to be said in favor of several different courses of action. Indeed, the variety of gifts that Paul mentions in 1 Corinthians 12 suggests that different Christians can be called to take different stances or supply different elements of a complex overall solution. (It would not be amiss, therefore, for another Christian group or a member of this group who met the black sheep in another situation to speak rather pointedly to him about the double-minded person condemned in James 1:7–8.) Overall the goal should be creating more and more positive situations in which people are helped to make the better choice or to fulfill the healthier obligation.

In this regard, I feel obliged to consider the work of fundamentalist and evangelical Christians. On the one hand, they very much want to exert the sort of influence I have been describing. They very much want to create an atmosphere in which marriage and family life will flourish and godless immorality will decline. Coming from churches that used to shy away from the social and political implications of the Christian gospel, they now quite commendably want to help their faith contribute to the politics of a better world.

On the other hand, the imperative that they apparently feel is not quiet the way that deep prayer and a level head suggest that it should be. Consider, for instance, the response of some evangelicals to the situation in South Africa.

The overwhelming reality there is the wrongness of apartheid. The first step toward peace and justice in that land, I feel, has to be repentance of this deeply evil political philosophy (and theology) and the full embrace of all human beings' equality. One should be patient with the complex process that transferring power will entail. Certain evangelicals have suggested that change often best occurs conservatively. But the prophetic imperative gives a radical spiritual evil such as apartheid no respite. One is patient with sinners, but merciless toward serious sin.

Similarly, the tactics of those who want to re-Christianize the American republic often seem hasty, simpleminded, and off the center of the target. The center of the target is the offer of Christ's good news, not an effort to compel people to accept that good news and a particular version of the ethical implications it carries. The more excellent way is actually helping unwed mothers, downtrodden people, children suffering on society's margins. To their great credit, the evangelical and Pentecostal churches often demonstrate this more excellent way vibrantly.

Is the biblical imperative to peace and justice indeed quiet?

Where might we find the wisdom to know the difference between what we can change and what we cannot change?

What are the advantages and disadvantages in the attempts of Christians to reform morality in the United States?

5

The Notion of Peace

Read Ephesians 2:11–22

When we speak of working for justice and peace, how ought we to understand the word *peace*? In my opinion, we ought first to think of harmony with God. For Saint Augustine, peace was the tranquillity of order, and order clearly came from God the Creator, Christ the Redeemer, and the Spirit who sanctifies us. From both biblical and pagan sources, fathers of the church such as Augustine thought of the world as legislated by God. Both nature and human events were fitted to a pattern laid out by the wisdom or law of their ultimate source. Modern science and modern political theory have forced us to rethink this basic conception of the relationship between the Creator and creation, but they have not brought us richer measures of peace. It remains true that unless we have accepted the mysterious primacy of God and fitted our wills to it, we cannot expect to have peace.

This description of peace may seem to focus on the individual's spiritual state, but a little reflection suggests that it applies equally well to the nations' search for the tranquillity of order. Until the nations come into harmony with the actual creation of which they are a part, we may expect them to keep on with their warfare and violence. The consistency with which the nations keep repeating their follies and blowing their opportunities to make the world prosperous in peace would be comic, did it not cause so much suffering. For example, scarcely a decade after the United States finally dragged itself out of its disastrous venture in Vietnam, the

Soviet Union was up to its elbows in a parallel venture in
Afghanistan. Neither democracy nor socialism, it seems, is
any sure formula for common sense and peace. Because
both systems depend on human judgment, both systems
regularly miss the mark and fail to gain the tranquillity of
order.

It is no accident, therefore, that both systems equally fail
to free themselves from the tyranny of the nuclear arms race.
As virtually all religious commentators intuit, the core of the
buildup of nuclear arms is the wrongheadedness of the two
great superpowers. They cannot work out a basis for trusting
one another sufficiently to start reversing the arms race, and
when the chips are down neither of them seems to want a
situation in which there are no nuclear arms. So politicians
and military analysts alike appear to write off the sobering,
compelling perspectives of writers like Jonathan Schell, for
whom the threat of nuclear war is absolutely the first problem
we must solve. Schell and his counterparts among religious
analysts are deemed "romantic" or "impractical" because
they think preserving the earth is more important than retaining
the ability to destroy one's ideological adversary.

In both our personal lives and our lives as citizens, the
view of peace offered us by Christian revelation and tradition
suggests the conclusions reached by humanists such as Schell
but gives these conclusions an instructively different rationale. For example, the Christian who takes scripture and
tradition to heart finally judges that human warfare and
antagonism derive from idolatrous hearts that refuse to submit to God's primacy. When we read the Bible with a
properly critical mind, letting the Spirit help us interpret
God's revelation in the light of historical experience, we find
that there is little basis for a doctrine of holy war. Just as
Jesus viewed the Mosaic legislation that permitted divorce as
a concession to the hardness of the Israelites' hearts, so we
may view the approval of bloody warfare that we find in the
Old Testament as a concession to the religious immaturity of
the Israelites of that period. If people joined in bowing their
heads before the mysterious sanctity of creation, they would
find two-thirds of their justifications for going to war swept
away. If God's life and love were our first treasure, we would

be much better able to negotiate differences over borders, raw materials, and political philosophies. It is true that this point of view most directly condemns the godless regimes that take only history or economics as their range of reality. It is also true, however, that very often the Western nations that have a different heritage act much the same as those nations that only bow to history and economics.

We shall come back to this central perception again and again, because all Christian discussion of peace and justice flows into and out from the primacy of the good God. In Christian perspective, political prosperity depends on right relation to a holiness and goodness that escapes the world. One may put this simplemindedly, as too many Christians who know only the letter of the Bible tend to do, or one may put it with all the lovely nuance and wisdom that a rich tradition of Christian intellectualism has assembled. The core truth remains: human life is disordered, and so is untranquil, unless people have their spirits opened to and formed by the creative mystery of God.

The applications of this truth in what we might call the psychological area of personal peace of mind are equally straightforward. There is no great puzzle in the upset and distress of people like the on-again, off-again member of the little home church. "Purity of heart is to will one thing," the great Danish religious thinker Søren Kierkegaard said, and this member impurely wills both God and mammon. Until God clearly dominates mammon in his life, he will know no bedrock peace. One would think that the shambles of his life and his manifest unhappiness would be sufficient evidence to convince him of this truth, but like many of us he is brilliant at fleeing from the obvious. Many of us know very well that money, pleasure, and power are false gods, yet we continue to pay them great homage. We envy the wealthy their plush homes and we think that the lusty intrigues of "Dynasty" and "Dallas" would make our lives much more interesting. Even when we entertain these notions half-humorously, think- ing about the troubles that running a big estate could bring or smiling at the trashiness of the life of a soap-opera heroine, the glitter of mammon has us blinking our eyes. American advertising and entertainment run by the glitter of mammon.

Politicians who do not arrive in stretch limousines or dress in high fashion rank low in the popularity polls. From the unhappiness of too many of its private citizens to the craziness of much of its foreign and military policy, contemporary America is an object lesson in what happens when people forget or ignore the one thing necessary. Without love of God with whole mind and heart and soul and strength, human beings can have no joy and peace. Without love of neighbor as self, human beings can have no settled, stable justice. These theological truths right from the preaching of Jesus may be hard to translate into economics and diplomacy, but in themselves they are embarrassingly simple. We don't miss them because they are too subtle or profound. We miss them because we don't want to be converted.

For the psalmist, only fools say in their hearts that there is no God. All people of sense and mental health know that they are neither the center of reality nor its most interesting member. Similarly, all people of sense know that nationalism, in the sense of exalting one's country above all others, is a pathetic venture in unreality. Nazi Germany carried its slogan "Deutschland über Alles" far enough to show any people with eyes to see that nationalism bears in its womb potent seeds of madness. Just as bedrock sanity and health of soul require our conversion from dreams of personal centrality, they also require our tempering of patriotism and ethnocentricity. One God means one Lord of All. One Creator means that all creatures have an innate dignity that we fellow creatures have no right to abuse. Take away the one God and any mad self-exaltation is permitted. Take away the Creator and it's no longer clear why nuclear devastation must not happen. Individually and collectively, human beings are marvelously intricate, exhaustively wonderful. Yet both individually and collectively, human beings have a very simple crux. Either they are made by God and so bound to be meaningful and valuable, or they are curious accidents of evolution who have no final rhyme or reason. We cannot separate the notion of peace from the choice set before us each day by Deuteronomy 30:19: "I call heaven and earth to witness against you this day, that I have set before you life and death, blessing and curse; therefore choose life, that you and your descendants may live.'' If we want life in the biblical sense of joy and peace, we must choose to love God above all else.

How is the ''order'' that Christian tradition associates with peace both like and unlike the ''order'' usually meant by the phrase law and order?

What is the idolatry at work in most military ventures?

Describe a properly Christian humor about television's soap operas and commercials.

6

The Requirements for Peace

Read Acts 15:1–11

I have suggested that peacemaking requires a heart or spirit converted to the truly mysterious God, and probably it would be well to ponder this suggestion more fully. First, let us reflect on the sort of personality that those who make peace at home or in the office tend to have. In the home the stereotype remains that Mom is the primary peacemaker. There are exceptions to this rule, of course, for sometimes Dad is the calming spirit (and sometimes no one cares for the peace). The notion in support of this stereotype is that something in upbringing or hormones tends to make women less prone to violence than men and more anxious to calm troubled waters. This would not be an unmixed blessing, of course, because there are conflicts that we have to face down or see through. Yet it has enough attractiveness in it, enough ring of deep sanity, that most religious traditions, including that of the Bible, have personified Wisdom as feminine.

So personified, Wisdom is too intelligent or subtle or skillful to think of solving conflicts by picking up a battering ram. In terms developed by the Taoists who greatly influenced traditional China, ultimate wisdom involves a lot of "not-doing" or "inaction." Why go to war and cause widespread slaughter when a bit of compromise here or a bit of flattery there could get the antagonistic parties back together? Why sacrifice one's children and lay waste to one's land when the sanity that speaks in the quiet of midnight leaves no doubt that most of our greed and egotism isn't worth murdering for.

The peacemaker who keeps the children from one another's throats or smooths the waters between child and
parent usually has this sense of the bigger picture. We all are
simply people and our lives are short. Do we really want to
spend precious time in combat with a blood-relation? Don't
we feel a rush of shame when we step back and compare
what we have been doing with what conscience tells us we
ought to do? None of us has ever seen God, so none of us has
the right to dictate all the details of what justice implies. All
of us, when properly humble, have to admit that other people
usually are not without some reasonableness on their side.

The peacemaker, in addition to being wise enough to help
the family stay in touch with the big picture, has also to be a
person who can tolerate diversity. In other words, genuine
peacemaking is not forcing everyone to say, do, or think the
same thing. The golden rule in Christian ecumenical reflection has been: in necessary things, unity; in doubtful things,
liberty; and in all things, charity. Often the family circle
seems like a bunch of bickering churches that are more
concerned about minutiae or rigid doctrine than they are
about the love of God on which they all depend. When a
matter of great moment occurs, certainly the family has to
pull together and act with one will. When the item under
discussion is relatively trivial, the rule of thumb should be to
let each family member do as he or she wishes (with due
provision for age and other responsibilities, of course). And
in all negotiations, discussions, disagreements, and spats, the
golden rule of charity stands as a chastening reminder. To be
right in one's opinion or reasonable in one's request is no
justification for acting uncharitably. Children and teenagers
will take some time to learn this rather key Christian teaching, of course, but adults should be quite hard on themselves
when they violate it. The "tough love" being preached in
some circles of Christian education today has its merits, but
those who would be tough on others ought to be even tougher
on themselves, making sure that their "charity" doesn't
camouflage self-righteousness or cruelty or manipulation. No
lasting peace will come from those.

When the religious get uppity about pagan disorder and
injustice, they might recall their own historical record. In

their bitter disputes and outright wars, the world's religions have given themselves little reason for boasting. One important implication of a proper appreciation of this history is that Christians should respect a spirit of peacemaking whatever its religious origins. For example, the Buddhists who have spoken eloquently of the need for nonviolence and peace should not be listened to only halfheartedly because they don't possess the revelation given through Christ. An ordered spirit, able to see the big picture and willing to work patiently to reconcile enemies, should be respected wherever found. For further example, reasonable critics of nuclear warfare who are determined to try to protect the earth's future children yet are not fanatical or full of hatred are a blessing whatever their religious or philosophical orientation.

One of the basic requirements for peace, in other words, is the ability to deal with concrete people and actual situations, not getting lost in rhetoric or dogma. Just as the weatherman who gives his report without first looking out the window is liable to be embarrassed, so the person who discusses peacemaking without providing for the nearly infinite variety of concrete positions that people actually hold is liable to be embarrassed. The experience of working together for peace, like the related experience of working together for racial justice, has brought many people, both religious and nonreligious, to respect points of view they previously had thought anathemas. As the great variety of signs and slogans of the marchers on national days for peace has suggested, wanting the tranquillity of order and seeing it as the fruition of one's dreams are very widespread phenomena. *Dialogue* and *ecumenical* are two words that now pale from overuse, yet the very fact that we can apply them nowadays to so many situations is testimony to considerable progress.

Consider, as a last example of the mind-set required for peacemaking, the current dialogue between Christians and Jews. In Catholic dioceses across the land, for instance, the twentieth anniversary of the decree of the Second Vatican Council on the relation of Christians to non-Christians has sparked programs focusing on Christians' relations with Jews. *The Journal of Ecumenical Studies,* which originally was conceived in an infra-Christian context and was concerned

with the movement to reunite the churches, recently has
sponsored several discussions of not only Jewish-Christian
relations but relations among all the traditions of the world's
religions. In the particular case of discussions between Christians and Jews, a great many grievances threaten to litter the
table. To be irenic or peacemaking in that context is to try to
summon the fullest possible measure of honesty about the
bitterness of the original break between Jesus' native people
and Jesus' first followers.

In a spirit of peace, with sensitive concern to nurture the
tendrils of good will that have grown in the past few years,
both sides have to deal gently with such questions as the
depiction of the Pharisees in the synoptic Gospels, the depiction of the Jews as a whole in the Gospel of John, and the
rightful place of the new nation of Israel in American foreign
policy. When it becomes necessary to disagree about particulars in these areas, Christians and Jews alike ought to fall
back on the heritage they share as believers in the one God
revealed in the Bible. Neither group can afford nowadays to
interpret the notion of election simplemindedly. Both groups
have to think that any "chosenness" they have is due entirely
to God's grace and meant more as a vocation to serve the
world than as a title to feelings of superiority. So, in religious
matters, as in matters within the family circle or among the
nations, humility emerges as the central requirement for
peace. I hope that liberation from sexual stereotypes will help
Christian men and women alike to appreciate how genuine
humility dovetails with spiritual vigor and strength.

How does peace usually come about in your family circle?
*What might be a Christian example of the "not-doing"
that the Taoists associated with ultimate wisdom?*
*How far might Christians' agreeing that Jews are not
"Christ-killers" and Jews' agreeing that the holocaust of six
million Jews by the Nazis was not a Christian undertaking go
toward making peace between these two religious groups?*

7

The Notion of Justice

Read Romans 5:1–11

The central idea in "justice" is giving all parties to a situation their due. The statue of Justice we find on many law buildings symbolizes this by holding a scale in which the two pans balance. Legal justice is also supposed to be blind, in the sense of ignoring the wealth or status of the parties to a dispute, so the statue usually is blindfolded. The religious sense of justice, which includes a large portion of mercy, is not blind. Religious justice reposes in the knowledge of God, the ultimate source of the world, who is able to factor in all the parties' motivations, backgrounds, and the like and come up with a judgment that is comprehensively fair. So religious people are caught in a demanding task. They must be blind to factors that would prejudice their interpretation of what fair-dealing means, such as in the matter of wages and monetary recompense. Yet they must also move beyond strict legalities and take into account the individual circumstances of the people involved in a given situation. Much of this second obligation Christians can fulfill by growing in compassion for all human suffering and weakness. To fulfill their obligation to support a fair-dealing that disregards improper privileges or influences of the status quo, they must strive mightily to connect their judgments of fairness with their (ideally powerful) appreciation of the primacy of the divine mystery.

To be more concrete, we might say that judgments about our American economy, if they are to be religious and

39

Christian, cannot assume that the haves possess the right to
continue to predominate and wax fat. There is nothing in the
gospel that defines *justice* as entailing the right of the wealthy
few to continue to enjoy luxuries. Indeed, the fathers of the
church tended to interpret the gospel as leading to the
proposition that no one has the right to luxuries as long as
anyone lacks necessities. In the eyes of the church fathers,
the supremacy of the One God renders all human beings
more equal than unequal. Consequently, all human beings
have at least the minimal right to a share of the goods of the
earth sufficient to keep them alive and truly human. This
minimal right comes before the right of anyone else to reap
profits from the earth that would allow a luxurious existence.
The fathers drew such remarkable conclusions from this
proposition as the right of starving or otherwise terribly
needy individuals to help themselves to the excess goods of a
person not in dire need. This teaching was no wholesale
attack on "private property," as we call it, but it was a
powerful statement of the equality and interconnectedness
that biblical faith finds existing among all human beings.

The "justice" that churchgoers find set before them as
their ideal will therefore be considerably more radical than
that legislated in many parliaments. If churchgoers contem-
plate the Pauline view of themselves as the Body of Christ,
they will find further reasons to take a deep breath. For the
Apostle to the Gentiles, who was concerned about the unity
of Christ's followers in a time when Jews and Gentiles sat
together only uneasily, the one Lord, one faith, and one
baptism that believers share make them not only members of
the same resurrected Christ but also members of one another.
They are involved in something organic that ideally they all
subserve. The pain or joy of one should be the pain or joy of
all. Paul's figure expands to utilize the common human
experience that pain in any bodily part, be it even the lowly
foot, affects our whole sense of well-being. The thesis being
exemplified is a unity that most of our conceptions of human
equality (and so most of our views of human justice) seldom
fathom: "Just as the body is one and has many members, and
all the members of the body, though many, are one body, so it
is with Christ. For by one Spirit we were all baptized into one

body—Jews or Greeks, slaves or free—and all were made to drink of one Spirit'' (1 Cor. 12:12–13).

Two recent books suggest the directions in which contemporary Christian thinkers have been taking these Christian instincts. *Human Rights in Religious Traditions,* edited by Arlene Swidler, places the Christian traditions' views of all human beings' basic rights in dialogue with the views of non-Christian religionists and humanists. *Human Rights: A Dialogue Between the First and Third Worlds,* edited by Robert A. Evans and Alice Frazer Evans, deals with cases for the Christian interpretation of justice that come from around the world (Nicaragua, Japan, Uganda, Australia, The United States, Switzerland, Brazil, and China). These books demonstrate quite clearly that working out problems of human rights, justice, and peace in a pluralistic or global context is a very demanding business. On the other hand, they leave the biblically informed reader with the sense that a living love of God could reduce most human conflicts to manageable proportions.

Justice in the sense of an eye for an eye and a tooth for a tooth is outmoded. These two books, like two hours spent with any week's Sunday *New York Times,* make it plain that a legalistic view of justice, let alone a punitive view that wants to exact vengeance to the fourth generation, is in today's world like a match thrown on ready tinder. Whether one is considering the Middle East or Northern Ireland, the tribes of Africa or the peoples of India, history has bequeathed us too many injuries on all sides. We can no more bring Turks and Armenians into a level relationship than we can bring English and Irish. Justice in the sense of a future free of past and present brutalities and hatreds requires a completely new beginning. Justice in any sense that Christ could accredit means being humbled and empowered by the divine spirit of love.

The justice for which the world groans, therefore, seems impossible. Set in the horizon of *The New York Times* or *Time,* people are no more likely to come into the dispositions that justice or peace requires than they are likely to sprout wings and fly. We have to respect this horizon, because it does spotlight certain regularities in human behavior and it is properly skeptical of miracles. But we also have to criticize this horizon, noting its disregard for the primordial fact of the mystery that we should exist at all and its neglect of both religious wisdoms in general and the Christian gospel in particular. The horizon that comes to us in the secular news makes little of grace, love, and saints. It goes deaf and mute before the cross of Christ, not with wonder but with puzzlement. Why in the world would anyone suffer for the sake of feckless human beings? At the least those human beings will not appreciate what one has done and often they will cheer as one is strung up.

And, of course, there is no reason in this world why the justice of Christ, the sense of fair-dealing that drove Jesus of Nazareth, came to climax on Calvary. Only the otherworldly love of Christ and his Father explains their giving the only begotten Son into the hands of sinners. What God found fitting so exceeds human beings' legalities that Isaiah's perception seems understated. As the heavens are distant from the èarth, so are God's ways beyond what human beings can appreciate. God's ways make it just, even necessary, that the Messiah should suffer and die. This theme is especially powerful in the Gospel of Luke, where the risen Christ fairly beats it into the two who encounter him on the road to Emmaus: "O foolish men, and slow of heart to believe all that the prophets have spoken! Was it not necessary that the Christ should suffer these things and enter into his glory?" (Luke 24:25–26).

The Christian notion of "justice" therefore tends to explode all human containers. When God makes determinations of what human beings are worth, of what fairness to any one of us can entail, we find ourselves confronted with the excesses of Calvary and the resurrection. It is as though the actions of the divine in time share in the hyperbole of Jesus' parables and moral demands. We are to forgive one another seventy times seven (endlessly) because there is no limit to the divine forgiveness and love. We are to take as our model the father of the prodigal son, who brushed aside the son's failures and rushed out to embrace him.

The core of our sense of how human beings should regard one another cannot be legalistic. We shall have to fashion laws if we are to live together well, but until we have animated these laws with a love worthy of the love shown us by the biblical God, our human communities will be no covenants worthy of our source.

What do you find the Christian doctrine of creation implying for a just distribution of the goods of the earth?

Was it indeed necessary that the Christ should suffer such injustice as crucifixion?

How can God ask us to set justice in the context of forgiving others seventy times seven or even of loving our enemies?

8

The Requirements for Justice

Read John 14:18–31

The love of God, excessive by human standards yet thrilling us with intimations of total goodness, provides Christians with their deepest sense of realism. If the force that made us and our world is loving to the degree that Jesus and the Spirit witness, then the way we usually look at the world and one another is crippled and straitened indeed. No doubt the deepest requirement for a justice that would honor the divine reality is our having hearts filled with the spirit of divine love. However, for the practical tasks of estimating what we from our faith can contribute to improving the state of the world, the renewal of our imaginations may be equally important. Let us therefore reflect on what such a renewal of imagination might comprise.

First, it certainly would comprise a fresh look at the images offered us by the scriptures. In the New Testament, for instance, Jesus is described by a wealth of titles and figures meant to express the newness that burst forth in him. The evangelists certainly saw Jesus as the fulfillment of Israelite prophecy or expectation, but they also sensed that what came in Jesus moved human existence to a plane beyond what even the greatest of the prophets, such as Isaiah and Jeremiah, had intuited. In terms that scholars of scripture often use, Jesus was the "antitype" who fulfilled beyond measure the "type" or first sketch fashioned in the Old Testament. So, for example, Jesus suffered along the lines of the Servant of God depicted in the songs appearing in the

44

Book of Isaiah. Yet the death of Jesus on the cross went deeper than the sufferings of the Servant, while the resurrection of Jesus raised both his own sufferings and the prophecy contained in Second Isaiah to a new plane. After Jesus, the evangelists found it clear that what Jesus the servant had taken upon himself was not just the sins of Israel but the whole revolt of humanity from God. Paul expressed this conviction by describing Jesus as the new or second Adam: the beginning of a fresh human line.

Similarly, the intuition of the prophet Jeremiah that when God's promises came to completion people would have new hearts and would be taught directly by the Spirit of God spurred Christian writers to think of the gift of the Spirit as a complete recreation of human nature. The seeds of this conception are richly scattered throughout the Gospel of John, especially through chapters 14 to 17. There the believer who abides in Jesus and the Spirit comes into a community of life with God. There faith so transforms human existence that eternal life, the quintessence of divine being, is given over to human beings and assures their immortality. What Jeremiah had sensed, from his faith in God and his awareness of what would have to happen for Israel to become worthy of God, occurred on a considerably higher plane. Jesus fulfilled the type or preview fashioned by Jeremiah, but so generously that the first impression seemed to the writers of the Gospels but a pale sketch of the later and actual reality.

Both sets of images, those that we can find in the Old Testament prophets and those that we can find in the pages of the New Testament, challenge us to rethink the relationship between divinity, the deepest mystery of human life, and human nature. Both sets of images say that the divine mystery communicates itself at the depths (what the mystics call the "fine point") of the human spirit. We tend to write the mystics off because we think them so special that our lives bear little relation to theirs. Yet the mystics, despite their special generosity and their special gifts from God, remain human beings like ourselves. What God does for the mystics is but a more intense degree of what God offers all human beings in grace. The deepest significance of "grace," as Eastern Christianity especially has stressed, is not God's

helping us lead tidy moral lives, but God's giving us divine
life. "Divinization" *(theosis)* is the complete fulfillment of
all human beings' desire for union with God. What the
mystics experience vividly and the rest of us only know in
special moments of dumb longing has more than been taken
to heart by God. If we will, we can become, in the words of
2 Peter 1:4, "partakers of the divine nature."

We shall not understand the riot of images produced by a
New Testament book such as Revelation until we grasp how
shaken and turned around the first generations of Christians
were. The resurrection of Christ blew apart their previous
conceptions of what was possible. Even though they were
devout believers who would no more have questioned the
existence and power of God than they would have doubted
the reality of sunrise and sunset, the first generations of
Christians found the resurrection and outpouring of the Spirit
shocking. What had but played teasingly in figures such as
Ezekiel's skeleton of dry bones taking flesh and breath had
swept through the world on Easter morning and Pentecost. In
the wake of the resurrected Christ and the paschal Spirit, the
vision of John of Patmos is almost expectable:

> I turned to see the voice that was speaking to me, and on
> turning I saw seven golden lampstands, and in the midst of the
> lampstands one like a son of man, clothed with a long robe
> and with a golden girdle round his breast; his head and his hair
> were white as white wool, white as snow; his eyes were like a
> flame of fire, his feet were like burnished bronze, refined as in
> a furnace, and his voice was like the sound of many waters; in
> his right hand he held seven stars, from his mouth issued a
> sharp two-edged sword, and his face was like the sun shining
> in full strength.
>
> —Revelation 1:12–16.

Now, the new imagery (or the redoing of Old Testament
imagery) that we find in the first canonical Christian authors
implies that any discussion of human affairs that we want to
have with them has to respect their conviction that a very new
thing had occurred in Jesus Christ. Old assumptions about
both God and human nature had been swept away by the
outpouring of God's Spirit upon human flesh. The images, of
course, did not remove the brutal or simply factual realities of

secular history. History did not literally end, people did not literally cease to die, and God did not once and for all wipe away every tear from the eyes of suffering people. Disease, death, sin, theft, injustice, rape, and all the rest continued to occur. On the other hand, none of these "fleshly" realities stayed exactly the same. All were cast in a new light because of the resurrection of Jesus and the outpouring of the Spirit. So the imagery of a book such as Revelation mediated, built a bridge, between painful existence in time and joyous, fulfilled, perfect existence outside of time (in "heaven"). Neither side of the bridge alone represented the whole story. To say that life was all gore flew in the face of not just the evidences of human goodness but, even more crucially, in the face of how God had cleansed life through and through in raising the Christ. To say that life was all grace, let alone all sweetness and light, also was untrue or unrealistic. The visions of John of Patmos and others like him took them into the realm of how things "have" to be in the perfection of God, but they were no literal reports. Revelation is not a heavenly guidebook written in the spirit of Arthur Frommer's early *Europe on Five Dollars a Day*. It is a poetic rendition of what the resurrection of Christ, embraced in faith, implies about human fulfillment, divine justice, and the like. Unless we balance it with scenes from daily life around our own specific neighborhoods, we shall join the too-large band of Christians who through history have missed the mark of biblical realism and come to wander in crazy illusion. Images such as those of Revelation are meant to break the stranglehold of a secular, unmysterious imagination. They are not meant to become a key to the hidden side of history or a prediction of what will happen in the year 2000.

As long as we retain proper sobriety and caution, however, we can only profit from steeping ourselves in the prophetic and apocalyptic imagery of the Bible. When we let these images carry our spirits toward the mystery of God, we break out of the barbed wire that condemns the secular imagination to hopelessness. Even better, when we let the Spirit take us beyond images into the simple being-to-being communion with God in love that preoccupies the masters of prayer, we find our hopes renewed and our sense of justice reset. However long it takes, God one day will fulfill human beings' most burning aspirations for justice. Because we have tasted the Spirit of divine love who serves as a down payment on the debt that God has voluntarily assumed toward us, we can pursue justice and peace quite matter-of-factly.

How do the resurrection of Christ and the outpouring of the Spirit reset the question of human nature?

How would you describe the experience of abiding in Christ or the Spirit?

What is a balanced, fully healthy view of the imagery of Revelation?

9

Peacemaking in Jesus' Image

Read Luke 11:14–26

The shalom that Jesus pursued was much more than the absence of armed conflict. To people steeped in the Hebrew Bible, the peace of God was a fullness of blessing and contentedness. Each Sabbath the people celebrated this peace. In separating themselves from workaday concerns, they strove to confess and enjoy something of the sovereign freedom that Genesis had in mind when it reported God's resting on the seventh day. New Testament writers, inheriting this tradition, understood Jesus to have freed peace, the Sabbath, and other Jewish notions from any too tightly legalistic interpretations. So Jesus is remembered as having felt free to heal on the Sabbath, as a better expression of the divine nature than a merely legalistic understanding of rest could be. Similarly, the author of Hebrews uses the figure of rest as a synonym for heaven, the realm to which faith promises to transport the believer. The peace of the Sabbath, the *Shalom Shabat*, plays in the earliest Christian imagination as part of the richness from which human strivings draw their interest and hope.

But how do the evangelists portray Jesus going about the work of making peace and drawing people into the rest of God? What is the main cast of Jesus' character and the main thrust of his teaching? Overall, the main cast of Jesus' character itself is peaceful. Jesus strikes us as a man almost above the fray of human anxieties and distractions. I say "almost" because the evangelists make it clear that sometimes Jesus did feel harried, sometimes he was bowed low

with fatigue. On the whole, though, Jesus moves through
space and time authoritatively, as one remarkably self-contained.
Just as he speaks crisply, with an authority and conviction
that the evangelists say amazed the crowds, so he does not
submit himself into the control of the crowds, and he never
worries very much about his popular reputation. Indeed,
Mark goes out of his way to depict how human opinion
turned against Jesus. Even the disciples hold back from
accepting the fact that Jesus had to suffer. Yet Jesus goes
ahead undeterred. The center of his life is God his heavenly
Father. To do the will of God is meat and drink, a source of
peace, far more important than public opinion.

So Jesus moves on the stage of the Gospels as a man at
peace with himself and with his God. Therefore, he can
relate well to other people and can often establish a harmoni-
ous, peace-filled connection with them. People flock to
him not only because he might heal their sick or enlighten
their minds. People also flock to him because he lifts their
spirits and makes their hearts burn with hope. The peace of
Jesus is quite energetic. We cannot separate it from the power
that would go out from Jesus when he worked at healing
sickness or casting out demons. In a figure dear to several of
the Synoptics, Jesus is like a champion who has come to cast
out the strong man presently holding a household captive. If
Satan is the strong man, and Satan's regime is bound to
trouble human beings' hearts, then the coming of Jesus is a
clear demonstration that the peace of God is stronger than the
turmoil of Satan.

The parables that Jesus uses to depict the growth of the
reign of God are another window into this powerful yet
peaceful presence of God that the evangelists want to describe as having arrived in Jesus of Nazareth. The reign of
God does not come like a violent storm (although in apocalyptic sections of the Synoptics the violent are said to be the
ones who bear the kingdom away). In the main, the reign of
God grows like a field in which wheat and tares coincide, or
like a mustard seed that begins small and then develops into a
huge tree. The kingdom is like a net cast into the sea that
drags up a great variety of fishes. Jesus is content, in other
words, to let the reign of God unfold as God sees fit.

Respecting human beings' freedom, he preaches and heals and prays with a patient, peaceful confidence that in God's good time the success God has in store for him will be accomplished.

This reminds us of the theme of necessity, which we saw in a previous chapter when discussing the Lukan sense that the Messiah "had" to suffer and so enter into his glory. It also calls to mind the Johannine interest in Jesus' "hour" of fulfillment. Jesus is concerned not to rush things or come to his final confrontation prematurely. He seems to sense an underlying rhythm or tempo with which he must try to stay in phase. Where a man of less judgment or a poorer sense of timing might have pressed too hard, Jesus seems regularly to have known just how far to go. In his training of the disciples, for example, one watches him plant the seeds of his conviction that he, and then they, will have to suffer. Then he waits for his word to take root.

There is, of course, a holy sort of impatience, and occasionally we catch glimpses of Jesus' longing to bring his task to completion. The saints who have tried to mold their love on that of Jesus also have flamed with a holy impatience, wanting to help poor people and sinners throw off their shackles. But the Petrine counsel to possess our souls in patience also bears remembering. In the mysterious counsels of God, salvation has not come as swiftly as the first generations of Christians expected. The Parousia has delayed, and because of that we have had to work out some accommodation with history and human weakness. Indeed, we have had as individuals to learn how to be patient with ourselves, letting God slowly fashion us into something before which we need not completely blush.

The image of Jesus at the work of peacemaking, like the images of Jesus at other of his central tasks, therefore comes into focus as a marvel of balance. The time is urgent and ripe, yet sufficient for each day is the evil thereof. The fields are ripe for the harvest, yet we should take time to consider the lilies of the field, how they grow. Jesus will be with us all days, through the middle of the marathon as well as at the more dramatic end. The proper stance of the Christian peacemaker is to straddle both "now" and "not yet."

Here and now, we can make considerable progress. Because of both grace and human freedom, we can expect to wash what has become dirtied, heal what has become ensored. Those who despair of human progress have no valid justification in the example or teaching of Jesus. When Jesus first preached in the synagogue at Nazareth, he declared that the prophecy of Isaiah had come to fulfillment, with the implication that his work of giving sight to the blind and liberty to the captive was more than possible: "The Spirit of the Lord is upon me, because he has anointed me to preach good news to the poor. He has sent me to proclaim release to the captives and recovering of sight to the blind, to set at liberty those who are oppressed, to proclaim the acceptable year of the Lord" (Luke 4:18–19). In the measure that they read this scripture with open minds and hearts, each generation of Jesus' followers felt empowered to do something right then and there to improve the lot of the suffering and spread the peace of the Lord.

The other side, which makes the equation balanced, is Jesus' sense that God stretches beyond any "here" or "now." If we have to criticize many religious people for dismissing the world and their here-and-now obligations, we also have to criticize those who would make Christianity just another movement of social reform. Christian realism, in the wake of Jesus, places perfection only in God and heaven. That God and heaven have burst into our human, temporal zone in the resurrection of Christ and the sending of the Spirit greatly expands our sense of what is possible when we believe. Yet orthodox Christianity never forgets that human beings have no lasting city here. Ideally, this frees them to work for justice and peace more realistically and purely than would be possible if they were driven by a this-worldly sense of perfectionism. Ideally, this removes the temptations that so often have led Marxists to try to root out imperfections and make heaven on earth by bloody spasms of slaughtering. In the peaceful way that Jesus assaulted human disorder, we have an exquisite image and model. Against all species of simplemindedness and haste, it bids us both love this world and love even more the world to come.

*What does Jesus' interpretation of the prophecy of Isaiah
61:1–2; 58:6 suggest about his understanding of his mission?
What place ought we today to make for God's sabbath
rest?
Explain what a balanced Christian this-worldliness would
entail.*

10

The One Thing Necessary

Read 1 John 4:7–21

The justice and peace that God revealed and established in Jesus stand midway between now and the time or state of fulfillment. They are "metaphorical," meaning things that are less literal and more pregnant with significance than workaday things tend to be. The justice of God is richer than what we can measure out onto the two pans of a legal dispute. The peace of God includes rest for the soul and satisfaction for hearts that have here no lasting city. So, like Jesus himself, these and other notions central to Christian life connote as much as they denote. Like Jesus himself, they are icons or sacraments that point the way to the mysterious simplicity of God. The one thing necessary in the spiritual life is that we keep opening ourselves to this mysterious simplicity. The only mortal failing is to close our souls and refuse to keep trying to hear what the Spirit is saying to the seven churches.

The seven churches, of course, are the fullness of the people of God. In the time of John of Patmos, they conjured up the relatively small and beleaguered bands of Christians that one could connect on a map of Asia Minor. In our time, the phrase should conjure up all people of honesty and good will, any human beings who honor the divine mystery that can manifest itself as the depth and allure of any decent reality or experience. Jesus is for Christians the sacrament of human beings' encounter with the divine mystery. His life and person have clarified what everyone born of woman is

54

about. He has overturned the flat, simplistic sense of "life" and "death," as Socrates also did. After Jesus, we have to estimate the success or failure of any person's life in more than worldly terms. The person rich in worldly accomplishments may be poor in wisdom and charity. The person considered of little account in the world may stand great in the eyes of God. Indeed, even this first bit of paradox has to be questioned, for further reflection makes us realize that poverty can twist people's spirits as well as their bodies. Good fortune can make people humble with gratitude. The more we ponder the one thing necessary, the more we realize that judgment, like vengeance, belongs to God alone.

If we push ourselves to stay open to the divine mystery and make its love our great treasure, we move outside the realm of any Caesar and attain at least the outskirts of God's rest. Whether our home is a shack or a palace, we always have miles to go before we sleep. If we fail by society's standards, entering the lists of the bankrupt or the fired or the sinful, we have not come to a dead end on our journey to God. Just as God can raise up children of Abraham, the father of faith, out of brute stones, so God can have further purposes for human failures. On the other hand, if we succeed by society's standards, we have still to account ourselves profitless servants. We have done only what was expected of us or what God's gifts to us virtually determined. The master may rightly make little of our accomplishments, knowing that full generosity would have begotten far richer successes. The one thing necessary is that we not settle down and presume to know exactly where we stand or what we are worth. Even when our hearts condemn us, God is greater than our hearts. Even when we see no progress or significance, ours is not the judgment that counts. With the apostle Paul, we must confess that we can never know whether we are justified in God's sight. Always we must believe in God and God's Christ, rather than trusting in our own merits.

More and more, I have come to think, serious spirituality walks the path of increasing surrender. John the Baptist caught much of this spirit when he gladly proclaimed that he had to decrease and Christ increase. In psychological terms, maturity means less egocentricity and self-concern. In philosophical terms, it means more objectivity. This objectivity is not unfeeling or impersonal. It takes away none of the wit and sparkle that we rightly love and find individualizing. Rather it makes us free like the dancer and the musician, who lose themselves in the objective reality of the music. Like the creative scientist, we should stand rapt before the complexities and beauties of a reality that colors us tiny. Like the Pauline mystic, we should live not for ourselves but for the Christ living in us.

It is hard to borrow these somewhat stock lines or figures without seeming to imply something grandiose. Yet the maturity I am praising is quite ordinary, gratifyingly commonplace. In two of the schools where I've taught, the secretary clearly had a greater measure of it than most of the professors. In several of the religious communities to which I've belonged, the brightest preachers showed less of it than the preacher with the least natural talent. People who take themselves to prayer on a regular basis and who try to examine their consciences so that they do not fudge the actual realities of their daily lives will usually find God giving them more and more peace and humility. People who are privileged to work with such prayerful types will confess, at least in moments of quiet and special honesty, that those people are the salt of the community—the main supports of fairness and the main sources of reconciliation.

For our given theme of peace and justice, this suggests that we make the bottom line a regular effort to be helpful. At home, at work, at church, our first job is to be a helper rather than a hinderer, a modest worker rather than a touchy supervisor. We may gradually become convinced that great changes in the current ways of doing business are necessary and so find ourselves revolutionaries of a sort. We may study the headlines, watch the news, and gradually come to think that we have to say no to the people and policies ruling our land. But even in these cases our Johannine posture should continue. Thus we will think it no big deal to change to another branch of the church universal or join a file of antiwar protestors. Such a move will not be a display of ego or a cry for attention. It will be but the next step in our daily effort to go forward a bit further into the mystery and apparent purposes of God.

If we love this sort of spiritual life—daily, modest, riveted onto the divine mystery—we may do virtually what we will. Saint Augustine is in the background here, of course, for I am but echoing his famous "Love and do what you will." Augustine's assumption is that if we love, we will do what is pleasing to God, the source and goal of our love. If we love under the impulse of God's Spirit we will freely take on the constraints implied in Paul's hymn to charity in 1 Corinthians 13. Love is patient, kind, long-suffering and the rest not because the lover has targeted these things, like lessons in an ethical primer. Love is the primordial force that makes any action moral and creative of good. Thus, people who love sometimes find themselves agreeing across political or ethical lines and then realizing how arbitrary many of these lines in fact are. "Liberals" and "conservatives," like "Protestants" and "Catholics," exist more clearly in textbooks than they do in reality. We are, of course, influenced by the schooling we have received in a given political or religious tradition, but if the spirit of God is alive in us, we are able to recognize kindred spirits from traditions we are "supposed" to find alien.

The one thing necessary can animate many different styles and conceptual systems. What it can never do is make people hateful or despairing. Love of the genuine, truly mysterious God always tells us that there are more things in God's power than our tiny list of certainties ever dreamed. Similarly, the charity that really counts always tells us to keep trying, even when this is in the mode of a counsel to let go and take what comes. The peace that surpasses understanding, like the justice that this world never gives, only comes into sight when we have surrendered ourselves enough to let God truly reign. The political life necessitated by the gospel is but the other side of the gospel's call to prayer. When we gaze at our suffering neighbors unblinkingly, we know that only God can change things to the depth they require. When we slip below words and desires and self-concerns, it becomes obvious that we have to try to love our neighbors as ourselves. This love is

the alpha and the omega. This love is what will prevail when
God is all in all.

———————————

*Can one be significantly human without loving the mystery
of God?*

Is humility a trustworthy sign of religious maturity?

*What political convictions does the peace of Christ tend to
foster?*

II

MAKING THE BIBLE CONTEMPORARY

11

Jesus in the Synagogue at Nazareth

Read Luke 4:16–30

We begin this middle section, where the task is a more direct focus on the lessons that the New Testament holds in store for people wanting to foster peace and justice today, by examining more fully a scene we have already glimpsed. The first two chapters of Luke, one recalls, comprise his narrative of Jesus' infancy. Chapter 3 brings forward John the Baptist, whom all the evangelists consider the precursor of Jesus, and it links John with Jesus by showing us Jesus' baptism by John and anointing (for ministry) by the Holy Spirit. Luke takes the lineage of Jesus back to Adam, showing the universal implications of Jesus' person and work. Then, in chapter 4, Jesus meets his first test: the temptations by Satan in the wilderness. Having conquered Satan (by a steady reliance on God's scriptural word), Jesus returns to his native area of Galilee and begins his full-fledged career.

Our text, Luke 4:16–30, is Luke's first chance to tell us how Jesus seems to have understood his work and what he regularly preached. Jesus goes to the synagogue at Nazareth on the Sabbath, is given the Book of Isaiah to read, and proclaims the moving words we have previously seen, verses 18 and 19: "The Spirit of the Lord is upon me, because he has anointed me to preach good news to the poor. He has sent me to proclaim release to the captives and recovering of sight to the blind, to set at liberty those who are oppressed, to proclaim the acceptable year of the Lord." After letting these messianic tidings sink in, Jesus tells the assembly that "to-

day'' this scripture has been fulfilled. For a Christian interpreter such as Luke, coming to the classical Israelite prophetic texts with a mind formed by the ministry and resurrection
of Jesus, what the prophet had described was but one of the
many messianic types that Jesus had fulfilled. The word of
God, always a source of liberation and consolation to those
who could not or would not put their trust in princes, had
come to marvelous, nearly unthinkable fruition in the good
news of Christ. The "acceptable year of the Lord," recalling
Israel's tradition of times of jubilee when debts were forgiven
and people could make a new start, was above all the *kairos*
or pregnant time during which Jesus had proclaimed God's
kingdom. Luke presents Jesus as well aware that his own
person and work are a fateful pause in the onrush of history.
What had been promised or longed for through the centuries
now could be attained: peace, justice, and true prosperity.
Above all, those whom history had sidetracked or disregarded
or trodden down were being presented a fresh chance. Consolation, release from prison, restoration of sight, and the
lifting of oppression all lay ready at hand.

Summarily, the Lukan Jesus begins his work with a pro-
grammatic claim that the time when God will reign and all
human affairs can come back into order is at hand in his own
presence. The people are said to have spoken well of Jesus
after this announcement, and to have wondered at the
graciousness of his speech. Immediately, however, they try to
cut him down to size. Is he not the son of Joseph, whom they
know (and probably don't consider extraordinary)? The implication is that, considering the source, they should take this
proclamation with a grain of salt. Jesus quotes the proverbial
literature and suggests that unless the people see signs and
wonders on their own turf, they will give vent to their will to
write him off.

Verses 25 through 27, in which Jesus reminds the crowds
that the powerful early prophets Elijah and Elisha worked
some of their greatest wonders for foreigners, are heavy with
Luke's sense that the church was forced to turn to the
Gentiles because Jesus' own countrymen had largely turned
him down. Luke is the evangelist most concerned to explain
the history of the church, and in that history the opening to

the Gentiles was the most dramatic happening. As with several of Jesus' pointed parables on the same theme (see, for instance, Luke 20:9–18), the suggestion that the kingdom or their chosenness may be taken from them fills the crowd with wrath. For the drama that the New Testament writers are presenting, the compatriots who will not accept Jesus' claims are the central villains. Here they rise up and try to do away with Jesus, prefiguring what will occur in Gethsemane and on Calvary. But rather mysteriously (in Luke the hand of Providence is quite heavy), Jesus passes through the midst of the crowd and goes away.

With bold strokes, then, Luke has shown us how Jesus understood himself and what his first hearers made of him. Jesus understood himself to be a "bringer of salvation," as some recent scholars of the New Testament like to put it. For Luke, Jesus felt that the time of healing and fulfillment had come. The kingdom was at hand. He also felt that the kingdom meant good news above all to the poor—the *anawim* whom Jewish tradition had closely associated with God's compassionate care. The poetic figures we find in the passage from Isaiah stand for a thoroughgoing set of blessings. That people would close themselves to these blessings could only mark them as dishonest or irreligious or perverted at heart. That they would take refuge in such trivial grounds for rejection as the fact that they knew Jesus' humble origins more than justified in Luke's mind Jesus' sharp criticism of them. Finally, that his early hearers would want to do away with Jesus when he suggested that their sense of chosenness could be challenged laid bare the murderous depths of their souls. As the author of John would put it (also early in his Gospel and as a leitmotiv):

This is the judgment, that the light has come into the world, and men loved darkness rather than light, because their deeds were evil. For every one who does evil hates the light, and does not come to the light, lest his deeds should be exposed. But he who does what is true comes to the light, that it may be clearly seen that his deeds have been wrought in God.

—John 3:19–21

When we try to bring texts of the New Testament to light, we already are attempting to make the Bible contemporary. Every interpretation builds a walkway between the cultural world of Jesus and the cultural world that the interpreter's readers inherit. The special edge that "contemporary" will have in this book is therefore but a small refinement of the regular task that biblical interpretation attempts. I want to suggest a Word cutting to the joint and marrow of our problems of injustice and warfare. The ax I have to grind would go to the roots of our unwillingness to share the goods of the earth fairly and live with one another peaceably. So what strikes me most forcibly in Jesus' first sermonic text is what apparently struck many of his hearers: the graciousness of the words of both Jesus and Isaiah said something that was beautiful and something that was hopeful. Indeed, they said something that was beautiful mainly because it was so hopeful. They could bring the mystery of God that must have been filling their own hearts to bear on the miseries people were suffering in their (or any other) times. They could raise the curtain that had come down on people's sense of possibility and reassert the freedom of God to make all things new.

"Grace" has many different connotations in the biblical religions, but all of them ferry hope and renewed possibility. The favor of God, when it anoints any person or time, is like light coming into dank darkness, like the bars of a prison cell falling down. In the time of Isaiah and the time of Jesus and the time of other historical epochs and our own time today, huge multitudes—perhaps a majority of humanity—have been poor and captive, spiritually blind and culturally chained. Jesus felt that he had been anointed by the favoring God and sealed by the empowering Spirit to preach—announce, herald, explain—the good news that this massive state of misery or wrongness or suffering does not have to be. If we will believe in the good news of a creative, redemptive God, repenting of our allegiance to such false gods as material security and spiritual cynicism, both the world in general and our own lives in particular can come aglow with goodness and cause for joy. That will be our theme through the reflections and practical ruminations that follow: It can happen, the world could become like Mary—hailed because full of grace.

In your experience, what excuses do people most often give for their refusal to take the gospel seriously?

How credible is Luke's portrait of Jesus' fellow Nazarenes as refusing to accredit his words because he was a hometown boy?

Why has the theme of election—first of the Jews and then of those who accepted the preaching of Jesus—been a bugbear in Western history?

12

The Samaritan Who Was Good

Read Luke 10:29–37

If our first sustained encounter with the New Testament context of justice and peace instructed us in Jesus' sense of his own mission, our second encounter sets before us one of the most influential models for Christian charity. The parable of the good Samaritan (Luke 10:29–37), like the parable of the prodigal son, has made Luke's reputation as the evangelist who most artfully renders Jesus' poetic teachings. It bears repeating that the story comes as an answer to the question of a "lawyer" or expert in Jewish Torah. The lawyer has just given the opinion that the love of God and neighbor is what the Law proposes as the way to inherit eternal life. Jesus has agreed with this opinion, saying that if the lawyer practices such love he will live. But the man apparently feels the need to express a sense of self-importance or to equate what he does as a Jew who observes the precepts of Torah strictly with the love that would gain him eternal life, for he presses Jesus to make precise the important word *neighbor*. Like a good Hasidic rabbi, Jesus answers the lawyer with a story.

The story is familiar to all who have grown up in a Christian church or have read the New Testament carefully. A man (presumably a Jew) was making a trip from Jerusalem to Jericho when he was attacked by robbers, stripped, beaten, and left for half dead. Two fellow Jews, a priest and a Levite (people who had special obligations to follow the Torah strictly), kept their distance from the wounded man and passed by. A Samaritan, who by upbringing could have been expected to despise a Jew, reacted differently. When he saw the unfortunate man, he was moved by compassion, dressed his wounds, and took him to an inn, where he cared for him. The next day he paid good money (a denarius was a day's wages) to the innkeeper to continue the man's nursing, promising that on his return he would pay the man's bill in full. Jesus concludes the story with a very simple question: "Which of these three, do you think, proved neighbor to the man who fell among the robbers?" The lawyer gives the obvious answer: The one who showed mercy on him. Jesus then drives home the practical significance of the story: "Go and do likewise."

At both ends of his interaction with the lawyer, Jesus is concerned with behavior: praxis. He bids the lawyer actually to practice the love of God and neighbor which the Torah makes central, and he tells him to imitate the good Samaritan in dealing with other people. When Jesus preaches or teaches, we may infer, the result he seeks is his listeners' behaving as the reality of the kingdom both invites and demands. No doubt loving God wholeheartedly and loving one's neighbor as oneself would always have brought "life" (a term as rich as it is vague), but in the time when Isaiah's acceptable year of the Lord had arrived, such love took on a special acuteness. The grace of the kingdom meant that categorizing people superficially as priests, Levites, Jews, and Samaritans was no justification for limiting the significance of *neighbor*. The prevailing interpretation of Torah gave the priest and the Levite some justification for avoiding the injured man. He could have been dead and so "unclean." The kingdom of God should make it possible for us to see through the walls human beings erect against charitable action, to break down the barriers by which we would make love and compassion neat and undemanding.

The Samaritan is depicted as acting spontaneously and naturally. He has no mental computer that he must consult. He comes upon a person who is in need and he gives that person help. Jesus has him move it right along: one, two, three. This briskness comes through in many of Jesus' stories, but in this context of Jesus' interacting with a lawyer,

Luke seems almost to underscore it. The lawyer perhaps
would have liked a scholarly discussion of the fine points of
the doctrine of love in the Torah. Jesus very simply says,
"Do this and you will live." The lawyer is a bit chastened by
the end of the parable of the good Samaritan, but even there
Jesus shuts the door on any further gloss: "Go and do
likewise."

I have spent many years in circles of religious instruction. I
have gained five graduate degrees, read many books, and
listened to many hours of scholarly debate. The relief I find
in Jesus' brevity and constant concern for the pith may be
somewhat unholy, but I am convinced it is also instructive. A
great deal of what is necessary for our peace and the peace of
the world is not obscure or complicated. We just have to stop
sitting around and do it. There is a time to search and study
and ponder, of course, but there is also a time to do it.
Scholars and lawyers become more hindrance than help when
they help us delay and fuel our will not to do it. The hue of
thought becomes sickly when it makes us afraid to act. A
great deal of the antagonism we can almost feel coursing
back and forth between Jesus and the representatives of the
religious establishment who oppose him comes from his
insistence that God wants direct, generous action. It is not
those who say, "Lord, Lord," who please God but those who
do God's will. It is not the son who promises that Jesus will
praise but the son who performs.

Recently we sold our house and arranged to rent it back for
two months before moving. The attorney who handled this
simple transaction seemed horrified that the woman who was
buying our house wanted no attorney of her own but trusted
us to get the exchange done. When it came to detailing the
terms of our renting, the attorney wanted to specify what
would happen if—the roof fell in while we were renting, the
basement flooded, the termites went crazy, and so forth and
so forth and so forth. "Enough, already," something in us
said. The one way to botch this deal, we knew in our bones,
was to destroy the bond of trust that our buyer and we had
established. If we followed a blind guide into the pit of
endless legal ramifications, we would all of us drown in the
mud.

The point is not, of course, that lawyers like ours don't have good grounds for trying to protect us against actionable damages. Every day the newspapers give us dozens of examples of litigiousness and conflict. The point, rather, is that such legalism as a dominant mentality undoes our humanity. When it controls us, rather than our controlling it, both common sense and wisdom fall apart. We become obsessed with rights and duties, both of which we tend to conceive quite narrowly. We become afraid to act and suspicious of every spontaneous overture (our own as well as other people's). We don't "do this," so we don't fully live. We can't "go and do likewise," because we feel naked without a map to guide us through all the details.

To an academic or a lawyerly mind, Jesus is bound to seem simplistic. Indeed, he may even seem dangerous. No doubt that is the reason that an evangelist such as Matthew, who seems steeped in the traditional Jewish veneration for Torah, goes out of his way to present Jesus as fulfilling the Law (rather than as abolishing it). Yet Jesus does, on any straightforward reading even of Matthew abolish the pretentions of the Law to be the measure of the divine love or the divine spirit. Jesus does throw down the gauntlet to lawyers and academicians, challenging them to show how their way is a better love of God or a better love of neighbor than his. I don't think they can do this, of course, and much of Western humanity has agreed with me. Jesus was not loved as the most compelling of human figures and venerated as the incarnate Word because he spun the nicest distinctions or marshalled the most cogent evidence. Jesus is the dominant figure of Western religious history because he spoke like a poetic sage and acted like a prophetic martyr. Above all, Jesus practiced what he preached—he did it and he suffered for it. "Therefore God has highly exalted him and bestowed on him the name which is above every name, that at the name of Jesus every knee should bow . . . and every tongue confess that Jesus Christ is Lord, to the glory of God the Father" (Phil. 2:9–11). Therefore, our concern for justice and peace has to be practical.

Whom does the Samaritan consider his neighbor to be?
In what sense is Jesus' way ruthlessly simple?
What can we do to get our laws from inhibiting our practical charity?

13

The Widow, the Mite, and the Temple

Read Luke 21:1–6

Throughout Christian history, Luke has been considered the evangelist who best captured the poetry and sensitivity of Jesus. From the lilies of the field to the prodigal son, the Lukan Jesus has eyes to see with, a heart to understand. Luke is the one who most stresses Jesus' bent for prayer (the best explanation for his sensitive awareness). It is in the Gospel of Luke that Jesus' sympathy for women is clearest. Many of these characteristics of the Lukan Jesus come together in the first verses of chapter 21:

> He looked up and saw the rich putting their gifts into the treasury; and he saw a poor widow put in two copper coins. And said, "Truly I tell you, this poor widow has put in more than all of them; for they all contributed out of their abundance, but she out of her poverty put in all the living that she had."
>
> And as some spoke of the temple, how it was adorned with noble stones and offerings, he said, "As for these things which you see, the days will come when there shall not be left here one stone upon another that will not be thrown down."
>
> —vv. 1–6

The rich don't get much sympathy from Jesus. He is not so simpleminded or world-hating that he equates riches with sinfulness, but he does think of riches as regularly impeding people's readiness to follow God's spirit. So, in the exaggerated speech that Jesus frequently uses, it is easier for a camel

71

to pass through the eye of a needle than for a rich person to enter the kingdom of God. If riches do not lead to an over-concern for this world's affairs, they lead to dangerous flattery and prominence in the community. Either way, they turn people conservative in a negative sense. Having so much invested in the status quo, rich people must work harder than the rest of us to see the evils in the status quo and fight for a justice worthy of God.

Jesus watches some rich people of his day put their perhaps quite handsome gifts into the treasury. The context is the area of the temple in Jerusalem, which was the center of Jewish life. A poor widow probably would not be noticed in such a context, except by a teacher who had a special love of the poor. Jesus interprets the woman's gift of two copper coins as an extremely generous donation. It may be trivial compared to the monies put in by the wealthy, but in her case it represents the best sort of alms. For, in Jesus' view, she is making over to God not part of her surplus cash but seemingly all of the small amount she has for food and shelter. Her gift therefore is a striking act of trust that God both will put her contribution to good use and that God will provide for her sustenance in ways she cannot presently predict. Jesus is moved by the woman's faith. As is regularly the case in the Gospels, trust in God brings a rush of love to Jesus' heart. One can imagine him saying something like what he says in other situations prior to working a cure: "Your faith has saved you." We are bound to think that this poor widow will be quite rich in God's kingdom. The gifts of the wealthy, although certainly they could have merit, move us to no such conclusion. The verdict is still out in their case.

The train of thought in this passage takes a turn and Luke moves on to focus on the temple itself. To counterbalance the admiration of "some" (probably some of his disciples), Jesus reminds them that even religious monuments cast in stone and glitter are bound one day to tumble down. At the time that Luke was writing, the shock of the destruction of the temple in 70 A.D. by the Romans was still reverberating throughout the Jewish world. Whatever reservations Jesus had expressed about the official religion that had centered in the temple were held in Christian circles to have anticipated this fall. Christianity also tended to think of Jesus himself as the new temple, seeing a parallel between the death of Jesus and the fall of the temple in Jerusalem. The crucial difference, of course, was that Jesus had been resurrected by his God. The lesson that Christians were bound to read out of this parallel and contrast was the greater surety of faith in Jesus. Where external cult and pride like that fostered by the temple proved extremely vulnerable to the ups and downs of history, faith in God like that of the poor widow or faith in Christ like that of the disciples who accepted his resurrection was virtually immune to attack.

The stimuli from these verses that we might seize upon for present purposes put together Jesus' sensitivity to the situation of poor people and the immaterial, imperishable center of a mature Christian faith. Jesus is more concerned with having people give themselves to God, center their whole lives in faith, than in having people hand over their money. The churches and shrines and temples that religious people erect no doubt have their place, but for Jesus they are all only corruptible instruments—things bound to rust and come unhinged, things only as good as the extent to which they help people love the mysterious God wholeheartedly. This point of view is, of course, devastating to the assumptions of much popular American religion. What is called "the electronic church," especially, does not square at all with Jesus' views. Insofar as that church, and in lesser degree most other churches as well, pressure people to ante up handsome sums for institutional purposes, they draw close to the profile of the established religion that Jesus seriously questioned. Insofar as a poor person who gave only a quarter would get little respect from a church's accountants, that church would stand prominently among Jesus' enemies. The horrible stories one reads of poor people, often the old or the sickly, being pressured by solicitations from the electronic church to the point that they feel besieged to give away money they desperately need show an utter perversion of Jesus' view of the widow. The energy and resources put into building glittering cathedrals sits badly astride Jesus' sense of the temple.

I am not saying that we should not have places of worship

and that we should not try to make such places beautiful. Anyone who takes the Incarnation to heart has to avoid such iconoclasm. That matter was hammered out doctrinally in the East to the victory of those who reverenced icons and insisted on the right of all creation to mediate the Creator's praise. It is reaffirmed psychologically every time that we catch the bad odor of puritanism and realize that a disrespect for beauty or the world or the flesh dishonors our God. I am saying that Jesus was very keen on the distinction between true and false religion. I am saying that Jesus was very hard on those who thought more of pomp and splendor and law than of the mystery of God and the needs of living, suffering people. Genuine religion, according to both Jesus and James, deals more with widows, orphans, and mites than it deals with wealth and ecclesiastical edifices. Genuine religion always feels that the time is short and the kingdom of heaven is at hand dwarfing all secular concerns.

One last inference that we can draw from this text is the legitimacy of religious consolation in Jesus' eyes. The widow presumably comes to the temple, to the house of God, because she finds there sources of peace and comfort that are in short supply elsewhere. Even today one who visits a large, dark, quiet church at midday is apt to find a scattering of people quite obviously seeking strength and consolation. I remember casually visiting a church at the edge of Metropolitan State College in Denver. We looked around, enjoyed the quiet, and then made our way back outside. On the way out, we passed a young woman sitting quietly with tears streaming down her cheeks. Whatever she had come with inside her was flowing out and I sensed she was half on the way to being reconciled to it. That scene now merges with dozens of similar scenes I have stored up from dozens of other churches. Students hunched over pews at midnight, old people lost in prayer—they all had come to the house of God to ask a help or render a praise they could not focus so well elsewhere. It is the faith in their venture that most counts, naturally, and they would not, if pressed, tie that faith inseparably to any building made of stone. Yet I think Jesus approves their instinct to seek out some religious precinct, just as he approved the widow's way of giving her mite.

How do you feel about almsgiving and tithing?
What advantage has the widow in the story over the rich?
What consolations may we rightly expect to find in church?

14

The Man Born Blind

Read John 9:1–41

Where Luke stresses the humanity of Jesus, John stresses Jesus' divinity. For John, Jesus is the eternal Word become flesh, so the life of Jesus is a series of "signs" that reveal the purposes of God. In chapter 9 of John's Gospel, we witness the cure of a man blind from birth. Woven into John's discussion of the controversy that Jesus' cure of the man on the Sabbath provoked is a remarkable stress on the honesty or straightforwardness that healthy faith manifests. The man who is cured is a pragmatist in the best sense, a person who accepts the facts and acts promptly on their basis.

The somewhat lengthy episode begins with the disciples and Jesus noticing a man blind from birth (perhaps he was a well-known figure or sat out on the public way begging). The disciples assume that such a state of ill-being as blindness ultimately derives from sin or wrong relation to God. Jesus says that things are more complicated than that, and that, besides, it is the present opportunity that the man represents that is the point. While Jesus is with the disciples, he is their light, and encounters such as this one with the blind man afford God a chance to show the divine power. So Jesus makes a little bit of paste from spittle and dirt, anoints the blind man's eyes with it, and has him wash in the pool of Siloam. (The symbolism here alludes to Christian baptism.) The man does what he is told and comes back seeing. As with the story of the good Samaritan, the action is direct and brisk. When his neighbors dispute whether or not this man who now sees once was the blind beggar they knew, the man settles the matter very simply: "I am the man." The onlookers ask how he got his sight and he gives the bare bones of the cure in a single sentence.

The crowd must be made up of busybodies for they insist on bringing the man to the Pharisees. John suggests the reason when he notes that Jesus had worked the cure on the Sabbath. The Pharisees ask the man for his story, and again he spits it out in a single sentence. The Pharisees then get into a convoluted debate among themselves as to whether Jesus is a sinner, because he did work on the Sabbath, or whether he is a man of God, because obviously he has exceptional powers. They cannot agree, so they ask the man who has been cured. "What do you say about him, since he has opened your eyes?" He replies, "He is a prophet."

This, too, is too simple for people who think themselves wise, so the Jews (John's terms for Jesus' unbelieving countrymen) interrogate the man's parents. The parents are afraid and so cautious: the man is their son, he was born blind, now he sees, and they know no more; he is an adult and can speak for himself. So for a second time the man is dragged in for questioning, and now his patience is being tried. The Jews demand, "Give God the praise; we know that this man is a sinner." The man cuts through this presumption: "Whether he is a sinner, I do not know; one thing I know, that though I was blind, now I see." The period that ends that statement comes down with a bang.

The interrogators try to rehearse once more how the cure occurred. The man will have none of that: "I have told you already, and you would not listen. Why do you want to hear it again? Do you too want to become his disciples?" This accusation of prejudice or dishonesty, combined with sarcasm, cuts the interrogators to the quick. They revile the man who used to be blind and puff themselves up as disciples of Moses. Compared to Moses this Jesus is a nobody. (Irony is always strong in John, and here the irony is that for John Jesus completely puts Moses in the shade.) The man born blind now gives them a full back-of-the-hand:

Why, this is a marvel! You do not know where he comes
from, and yet he opened my eyes. We know that God does not
listen to sinners, but if any one is a worshiper of God and does
his will, God listens to him. Never since the world began has
it been heard that any one opened the eyes of a man born
blind. If this man were not from God, he could do nothing.

—9:30–33

This outburst only wins the man more contempt, for the
"teachers" are infuriated that he should assault their authority. They cast him out of their midst, and perhaps out of the
synagogue (religious community). Jesus seeks the man out,
solicits his faith in himself as the Son of man, and wins the
man's worship. John concludes the episode with the following exchange between Jesus and some Pharisees:

Jesus said, "For judgment I came into this world, that those
who do not see may see, and that those who see may become
blind." Some of the Pharisees near him heard this, and they
said to him, "Are we also blind?" Jesus said to them, "If you
were blind, you would have no guilt; but now that you say,
'We see,' your guilt remains."

—9:39–41

The Isaian theme that God's word seems to turn some
people deaf and blind takes the Johannine turn that Jesus was
a crux determining people's good will. Those open and
humble rejoiced in the light that Jesus shed. Those closed and
presumptuous could make nothing of it (indeed, hated its
challenge).

I have long loved the Gospel of John, and the man born
blind is probably my favorite character in it. He is a splendid
model of faith. There he sits, living a life burdened with a
horrible affliction, and Jesus comes along to turn him around
180 degrees. He is cured, the story suggests, because he is
willing to do what Jesus tells him. He may have said to
himself, "How can it hurt?" Or he may have been deeply
moved by something in Jesus' manner that the story doesn't
stress. Either way, the man is utterly realistic: here I am, this
has happened, I'd best respond. The man then puts up with
the fussy attention, interference, and interrogation of his

neighbors and the religious authorities. When he sees that the point of all this attention is not to determine the truth but to try to attack Jesus, he blows his interrogators out of the water. For this he suffers their further abuse, yet in John's story he is clearly the stronger personality. Not only does he stick to the straight facts of what has happened, he reads out of these facts the obvious interpretation: God has been at work. When he meets Jesus, he fills out this interpretation with a formal act of faith. The Johannine program, which rests on the connection between deeds or signs and saving faith, is all there in a nutshell. Jesus has done deeds that any honest interpretation will consider warrant for full commitment to Jesus' God. Faith is badly served, truth is greatly dishonored when tradition or pride or any other hindrance to our straightforward analysis of what happens to us is short-circuited. An honest mind and a pure heart don't falter when it comes to drawing even demanding consequences from the truth.

This Johannine pragmatism dovetails with Jesus' own criterion for the assessment of religious claims. In both the synoptic tradition and the Johannine tradition, Jesus uses "fruits" as the test. We can know the value of both people and concepts or intellectual positions by the fruits they produce (the actions and consequences that flow from them). If nothing practical happens or results opposed to God (hatred, injustice, strife) develop, we should hold both the preacher and the preaching suspect. If we see bickering and over-analysis and holding back from the obvious inference, we should suspect a feeble or twisted faith. When people cannot bear to see the light and to walk the path that the light discloses, they fail the evangelical test. We have to be cautious in dispensing judgments here, as everywhere, but we also have to remain hardheaded. Christian faith occurs in the world, on the basis of actual experience, and it either issues in practical actions or it is dead. In Johannine terms, if we profess to love God while we hate our neighbors, we are liars. If we see a brother or sister in need and close our hearts, we have no love of God. The man born blind came to a dazzling realm of light because he could be thoroughly honest. Many people given all sorts of advantages end up

with dismal souls because they are afraid or unwilling to go
and do likewise.

What is the relation between sin and disease?
How could the man who had been blind be so courageous?
What is the proper sense in which Christian faith is very
pragmatic?

15

Zacchaeus Up in the Tree

Read Luke 19:1–10

Another character in the New Testament who has amused
me and gained my admiration is Zacchaeus, the little tax
collector whose encounter with Jesus is described in Luke 19.
Once again Jesus is passing along when his chance encounter
with a bystander changes that person's life. Zacchaeus, however, in contrast to the man born blind, is no simple object of
pity. His position as a chief tax collector of his area has made
him rich. The price he has had to pay, however, is the
contempt of his fellow Jews. They see him as a tool of the
hated Roman rulers (for whom he collects the taxes), and
religiously he is lumped with the prostitutes and other public
sinners as unclean.

Zacchaeus wants to see Jesus, about whom no doubt he
has heard much gossip. But he is a small man and so cannot
see over the crowds. That he has gained his riches and
authority by enterprise is suggested by the quick action that
he takes. Running ahead of the crowd, he climbs up a
sycamore tree to get a bird's-eye view. Jesus sees him up in
the tree and (inexplicably, apart from Luke's theme of providence) tells him to hustle down and get his house ready so
that Jesus can stay with him. The implication is that Jesus
read in Zacchaeus' initiative and effort at least the seeds of
faith.

Zacchaeus, like the man born blind, obeys Jesus' behest
decisively. Indeed, Luke says that he made haste (I see a little
man shinning down, somewhat out of breath) and received

Jesus joyously. But the people in the crowd, who as in the story of the man born blind have too little to do and too much to say, murmur disapprovingly. One gets the impression that they included many busybodies who were just waiting to find something in Jesus' behavior or teaching that they could criticize. In this case they are condemning Jesus for consorting with a "sinner": a person impure or unclean by the Pharisaic interpretation of Torah.

Zacchaeus, quite sensitive when it comes to public opinion, confronts this reaction straightforwardly. He tells Jesus that he gives half his goods to the poor (an extraordinary generosity), and that if he has defrauded anyone of anything (made a mistake or been unjust in his work of taxing), he restores it fourfold (there is an allusion here to the laws for recompense in Exodus 22 and Leviticus 6). In other words, this "sinner" in fact leads a life of exemplary justice and charity.

Whatever Jesus discerned in Zacchaeus up in the tree, the man who is serving as Jesus' host more than justifies the Lord's visitation. Jesus confirms this impression with the moving words, "Today salvation has come to this house, since he also is a son of Abraham. For the Son of man came to seek and to save the lost" (vv. 9–10). Jesus may seem to accept the categories of his opponents, according to which Zacchaeus was a sinner or one "lost," but in fact the key point is that Zacchaeus (rather than the religiously pure) has proved worthy of salvation (the visitation of grace). It is such as he—people despised by ordinary society or passed over by history yet still honest at core—that the Son of man (the splendid figure of Daniel 7 and the most fully human or representative of human beings all wrapped in one) has come to make whole.

Zacchaeus, like Mary Magdalene, represents Jesus' outreach to people whom the religious establishment of that day condemned. If the religious establishment had owned condominiums, it is the Zacchaeuses and Marys that they would have been after the police to roust. True, Zacchaeus was wealthy, but wealth means little if one is constantly exposed to public contempt. And it must have frustrated Zacchaeus, even if his motives in being charitable were of the purest, that what he actually did in his work and life could so little counteract the social judgment passed on him because of what he was (or was thought to be: his pigeonhole). Once again we see the damnable presumption of legalism and the reason that so much of Jesus' preaching about the kingdom boiled down to overthrowing popular assumptions. When God is alive very few things are certain. Most of reality is flexible and can move its significance in a twinkle, because its crucial significance depends on its relation to God. The few things that are certain derive from the divine mystery: We really can entrust ourselves to reality; we really can live on a bedrock of peace and joy. All other things are largely in the eye of the beholder, which very often is beam-ridden and bloodshot.

For our purposes, it is worth beating a bit on the obvious point that Zacchaeus's basis for defending himself against the popular judgments made upon him was his charity and exactness in money matters. He was extremely generous to the poor—openhanded to a degree far more likely attributable to a genuine compassion for the poor than to superficial or even substantial guilt. It clearly was a point of honor with him to conduct the always burdensome business of taxation scrupulously. We are not told how he got into the position of being a tax collector and so an agent of Rome. Other sayings of Jesus in the context of Roman rule and taxation, especially the famous "Render to Caesar the things that are Caesar's" (Luke 20:25), suggest that Roman rule was not for Jesus the utter abomination that it was for many Jews—largely because Jesus took the whole secular or political realm less seriously than they did. What we do know about Zacchaeus is that despite his occupation, he labored on the side of the angels. If all tax collectors had gone about their business as he had, there would have been relatively little room for grumbling. Similarly, if all observers of Jesus had been as open and energetic as Zacchaeus, the kingdom would have advanced more dramatically.

The Son of man, come to save the lost, is bound to esteem matters such as taxation as secondary. Equally, he is bound to be more impressed by a ready faith and a generous charity than by standoffish judgments about purity and sinfulness. I think of this second characteristic regularly, because regularly I find all around me (and in myself) assumptions and judgments that are in fact much more arbitrary or provisional than God likely considers them to be. For example, as I find myself frequenting the branch of the local supermarket chain that caters to the upper crust and shying away from the other store nearby where the winos and street-people gather, I wonder what I am in fact saying. On the first point, the matter of the significance of taxation, I think of the massive industry that we have made of taxation in our country and of the seriousness with which we approach it.

The churches have not escaped this seriousness, as an article in the diocesan newspaper of the city where I grew up reminded me recently. The superintendent of the parochial school system, a man whom I knew in our high school days, was expressing "outrage" that government support for nonreligious subjects taught in religious schools would, under a new interpretation of the separation of church and state, no longer be available. I have been interviewed by papers enough to know that what appears in the headline often is quite different from what transpired in the interview, but I still found the quoted words unfortunate. They suggested a degree of preoccupation with funding and public approval that doesn't square with genuine Christian religion. The basic business of religious schools ought to be excellent education in all subjects with which they deal. If the public at large will support their venture, so much the better (by and large; public support also has its drawbacks). If they are being discriminated against, they certainly should fight such evil, but seldom to the point of spilling away their peace in the realm of the news media. Especially, they should keep a healthy distance from the mentality that sees education or religion as but another business, as though the financial balance sheets had a direct correlation with spiritual progress.

Jesus bids us be concerned with spiritual progress and God's grace, so that we handle matters of business and taxation with little ado. Jesus was sufficiently free of concern about such matters to deal with people on both sides of the economic ledger. What concerned him was neither a person's bank account nor a person's legal rectitude. What concerned Jesus was a person's need and a person's faith.

Compare the psychology of faith that we see at work in Zacchaeus with the psychology of faith that we found in the man born blind.

How do you think Jesus would define the word sinner?

What would be the basic theses one would have to develop in writing a Christian theology of taxation?

16

Obeying God Rather than Human Authorities

Read Acts 5:12–32

In the fifth chapter of Acts, we glimpse yet another aspect of the somewhat complicated Christian view of authority. Zacchaeus, representing the taxing power of foreign Roman rulers, was despised by the Jewish orthodoxy of Jesus' day. Yet that orthodoxy, in turn, wanted to lord it over the people subject to it, as the Christian orthodoxies that have dominated the later centuries frequently have wanted to. The conflict in Acts 5 is between the rights of the first followers of Jesus to preach the good news of his salvific death and resurrection and the rights of the Jewish religious leaders to stamp out preaching they thought heretical or dangerous. Out of the mouth of Peter, the leader of the little Christian community that had gathered in the upper room after Easter and been dramatically energized by Pentecost, comes the line that has echoed throughout subsequent Christian history, furnishing great varieties of protestors and reformers with one of their cardinal tenets: "We must obey God rather than men" (v. 29). Let us first place this verse in context and then reflect on its further significance.

The apostles have been preaching about Jesus in the temple and so have incurred the wrath of the high priest and religious leaders. They have been put in prison, but at night an angel of the Lord has let them out and recommissioned them to preach: "Go and stand in the temple and speak to the people all the words of this Life" (v. 20). So the apostles have gone back to their stand, much to the chagrin of the Jewish leaders. These leaders were vexed enough to find that their prisoners had escaped, but to find them completely unrepentant was outrageous. So once again Peter and the rest are hauled by the police back before the high priest and the Jewish council. The exchange between Peter and the high priest suggests both the priest's irritation and Peter's boldness:

> "We strictly charged you not to teach in this name, yet here you have filled Jerusalem with your teaching and you intend to bring this man's blood upon us." But Peter and the apostles answered, "We must obey God rather than men. The God of our fathers raised Jesus whom you killed by hanging him on a tree. God exalted him at his right hand as Leader and Savior, to give repentance to Israel and forgiveness of sins. And we are witnesses to these things, and so is the Holy Spirit whom God has given to those who obey him."
>
> When they heard this they were enraged and wanted to kill them.
>
> —Acts 5:28–33

Cooler heads, represented by the respected teacher Gamaliel, prevail, so the apostles get off with another warning and a beating. This hardly deters them, for in fact they rejoice that they have been found worthy to suffer dishonor for the name of Jesus. "And every day in the temple and at home they did not cease teaching and preaching Jesus as the Christ" (5:42). The apostles, we may say, were convinced that they had an obligation in conscience to preach the gospel. Since obeying the religious authorities would have been disobeying this obligation in conscience, they had no choice but not to obey the religious authorities. By comparison with the events they had witnessed and the interior inspirations they had received, the voices of the religious authorities were but limited, very human things.

The apostles must have felt that the high priest and the religious leaders had done damage enough in arranging for Jesus' death and crucifixion. They must have felt that such religious authority continued to disqualify itself by its prejudice and closedness. It is worth noting that the apostles did not oppose the Jewish religious leaders violently. They let themselves be carted off to prison and they had to suffer a beating (to be lashed was no pleasant experience). But, like Gandhi before the British, they were uncompromising in spirit. Tough as nails when it came to what they considered the new truth that gave their lives immeasurable significance, they did diametrically the opposite of what their official bosses (they were still Jews, and so still subject to the Jewish religious authorities) had commanded them.

This text and our ruminations have, of course, brought us to the border of a tangled underbrush. Precisely how to balance off the rights of individual conscience with the needs of the community at large for order and cohesiveness is a problem that, on the historical record, we can never completely solve. Catholic Christianity has tended to be like the Jewish leaders, wanting to silence any preacher it has considered heretical. Protestant Christianity has, in the phrase of Robert McAfee Brown, found authority to be its Achilles' heel, with the result that it has splintered time after time. The secular authorities of the United States have in recent decades fitted themselves to the profile of the high priest and his council, being slow indeed to see the justness of the protests for civil rights and American disengagement from Vietnam. On the other hand the protestors, both religious and purely secular, often have seemed to fail to appreciate the claims that duly elected leaders should be able to make on citizens in the name of the common good. The issues in these conflicts have ranged from the most profound to the quite trivial, but throughout, the old problem of the one and the many has kept perplexing us. How can any community strike just the right balance that both keeps its members truly united to one another, so that they are in fact a community, while it also allows them to be sufficiently free as individuals to express themselves and pursue the fullest possible measure of God's truth (which of course in return will greatly enrich the community as a whole)?

The "answer," if we may call it that, to most questions such as this is to develop an atmosphere in which both sides or parties go 60 percent of the way and look out for one another's interests. If Catholic church authorities had considered the rights of individual Christians' consciences a very great value that they were bound to protect and promote, while Protestant reformers had bent over backwards to cherish and preserve the union of the Body of Christ, the Reformation probably would have occurred without most of its very damaging aftereffects. If American political leaders had cared more for the truth that the protestors in the era of the civil rights and anti-war movements were elucidating than for political power plays, while the protestors had been kinder and more sympathetic toward the conservative sort of patriotism that finds it hard to make quick changes, the American decade 1965–75 would have had considerably less shame and suffering. One could draw analogies to other instances of community life, including even the life of that little community called the family, and in almost all instances the "answer" equally would emerge as a matter of mutual concern or responsibility for both the one and the many.

I must also say, however, that the principle that Peter and the apostles finally enunciate when it comes to the crunch and reconciliation appears impossible very much remains the bottom line. We must obey God—what we know in our hearts from prayer and the most rigorous self-examination—rather than human authorities who would force us to go against God. Regardless of what supposed orthodoxy is telling us, if we are convinced in conscience that something else is God's truth or will, we have to act upon our conviction (and suffer the consequences as the apostles did). As I write, the most brutal example of such a conflict is being beamed to us from South Africa. The laws of apartheid (and the laws that would prop apartheid up) show the depths of perversion to which legalism can go. In South Africa, as in Nazi Germany, to act upon one's religious convictions often results in finding oneself illegal—a criminal according to the government's code. One can and should try to obey God prudently, of course, not risking the destruction of one's self or family foolhardily. But in the crunch, we have no choice but to fit ourselves to the model of Christ and suffer the consequences. In the crunch, therefore, it again becomes clear that Christians have in this life no lasting city. What we profess to believe is only justified or given the context that makes it fully rational in the kingdom of God that is fuller than history.

———————

Explain why the high priest and the Jewish council thought the apostles should have obeyed them.

What are the worst dangers in insisting on the supremacy of individual conscience?

How ought we to examine the inspirations or the teachings that we or others are claiming express the will of God?

17

The Place of Civil Religion in Romans 13

Read Romans 13:1–7

In counterpoint to the exclamation of Peter and the apostles in Acts 5, the voice of Paul in Romans 13 seems to stress the rights of the governing authorities. Ultimately, of course, Paul too would hold that one must obey God rather than human authorities. In fact, Paul's own preaching of Jesus put him on the outs with local Jewish authorities in town after town. But in Romans 13, he is reflecting on the way that the one God, whom Paul certainly considered to be quite directly in charge of both nature and human affairs, has chosen to employ state authorities (with their armies and their tax collectors and the rest).

The first assumption that Paul makes is the tip-off to his conviction that God is immediately at work in affairs of state or daily politics: "Let every person be subject to the governing authorities. For there is no authority except from God, and those that exist have been instituted by God. Therefore he who resists the authorities resists what God has appointed, and those who resist will incur judgment" (vv. 1–2). In other words, human beings need laws and officers if they are to live together in justice and peace. When people so violate the duly constituted order of secular life that they and their principles would render decent human community impossible, they show themselves to be out of phase with God's plan of creation. I have added the words "duly constituted," which do not occur in Paul's own writing, to fill out another assumption that I think Paul is making. Unless we want to make Paul the blind support of any might that is claiming the right to rule, we have to add that political rule derives its legitimacy from its consonance with the divine standards of fairness, and from the consent of the governed.

It is interesting that Paul implicitly lets the first consideration—overall consonance with the divine standards of fairness—outweigh the second consideration. That is, it is interesting that the fairness of Roman rule, overall, weighed more heavily than the agreement or consent of the population (for example, the Jews) being governed. Certainly the Jews despised Roman rule and would have voted for their own autonomy. (In the actual case of their subservience to Roman rule, however, many Jews advocated compromise and accommodation with the Roman authorities.) This seems to mean that Paul somewhat accepted the hurly-burly of history according to which one regime succeeds another and smaller powers regularly get dominated by greater powers. If so, the likely explanation is that Paul, like Jesus, was relatively indifferent to matters of political regime. All either prophet asked of the secular authorities was that they keep the peace and let the people concentrate on such central things as the kingdom of God or the gospel of Christ.

Paul's second assumption is that the rulers of the apparatuses of the state on the whole are fair, so that their punishing someone as a criminal is a pretty good sign that that person has done criminal things:

> Rulers are not a terror to good conduct, but to bad. Would you have no fear of him who is in authority? Then do what is good, and you will receive his approval, for he is God's servant for your good. But if you do wrong, be afraid, for he does not bear the sword in vain; he is the servant of God to execute his wrath on the wrongdoer.
>
> —vv. 3–4

This, too, needs some amplification if it is not to open the door to great abuse. The mere fact that civil authorities—police, mayors, governors, bureaucrats—take exception to one's activities is no guarantee that one is on the outs with God. Paul passes over the whole matter of the corruption of civil authorities, of which we have had too many examples both throughout human history as a whole and in recent United States experience. The sticking point usually is where a citizen would protest the policies of the state or civic unit and so shine a light on an injustice or prejudice that the authorities themselves want to continue. One thinks of brutalities against blacks that white authorities have spearheaded, or of ways that Richard Nixon and his circle of inner counselors wanted to use the FBI and the IRS to harrass those who opposed their policies.

Rulers on the whole indeed are not a terror to good conduct, as long as that "good conduct" does not include prophetic protest against unjust government policies. But if the commandment of God, ringing in inner conscience, should lead one to public protest against systematic racial or sexual injustice, against the buildup of nuclear arms, or against one's country's support of murderous foreign dictators, the wrath that comes down certainly should not automatically be assumed to be God's punishment. More likely, it is the cross of Christ that one is experiencing, and one should be consoled to recall that, according to the evangelists, Jesus went to his death as the victim of corrupt authorities, both religious and civil.

Paul's third proposition is less problematic. He follows up on the claims that civil authority can make on citizens' consciences (when it is healthy), and then draws the practical conclusion that citizens must comply in the ways necessary to keep the civic order functioning: "For the same reason you also pay taxes, for the authorities are ministers of God, attending to this very thing. Pay all of them their dues, taxes to whom taxes are due, revenue to whom revenue is due, respect to whom respect is due, honor to whom honor is due" (13:6–7). To be sure, this advice is rather blank or in need of further specification, like the advice of Jesus himself. For just as "Render...to Caesar the things that are Caesar's" begs the further question of exactly what Caesar's things are, so the advice to honor those to whom honor is due raises further questions about what is honorable office or behavior. Nonetheless, Paul clearly thinks that taxation and subjection to civil power is in itself unobjectionable. It certainly can become excessive, but in the Pauline view of things, there is no justification for an ultraindividualism such as that of some political radicals or of the *posse comitatus* groups who in effect despise the powers of the civil order.

The liberation theologians who have arisen in the past generation, mainly under the influence of the sufferings caused by oppressive political regimes in Latin America, probably would make a sharper qualification of Paul's teaching in Romans 13 than I have, but I doubt that the mainstream of them would deny that when a civil authority is just, genuinely trying to serve the common good, we do well to think we have an obligation in conscience to obey it as a power sanctioned by God. Similarly, all but the most extreme representatives of black, feminist, Asian, African, and other schools of liberation theology would agree that in itself civil authority should be a blessing. The problem tends to come, they would say, when such authority does not represent and serve all the people but is rather, in effect if not conscious intent, the tool of only particular and favored classes.

Such a judgment certainly inclines many liberation theologians to be sympathetic to political socialism, in the sense of a form of government that would truly represent all the people and work for the good of the populace as a whole. But it does not necessarily mean that liberation theology must be considered Marxist. Marx certainly can be read in support of socialism as we have just defined it, but the Marxist regimes that have come to power in the Soviet bloc and East Asia by no stretch of the imagination can be considered forthright servants of their entire populaces. In addition, the means by which they frequently have chosen to impose their will are often so brutal and inhuman as to destroy any claim one might make that they are simply representing God in the realm of civil affairs. Like the brutal conditions and attitudes in place in many Latin American regimes that are allied with the United States, the sinfulness of the "Marxists'" means has destroyed their claims to authority. The terrible irony, of course, is that when the labels *Marxist, Communist, Democratic,* or *Capitalist* are peeled off and we look at bare performance, at the real fruit by which to judge, so many regimes supposed to be diametrically opposed to each other turn out to be nearly equally rotten. So we have to fit what Paul says in Romans 13 to what Jesus says in Matthew 7 and Luke 6: We can know any regime or lifestyle by its fruits.

Does Paul seem to tie secular affairs to divine providence more directly than today's Christians tend to do?

What should we think and do about civil authority that seems to be part of the problem of injustice and warfare?

Should the state, as a legitimate expression of divine authority in the civil realm, possess and exercise the right to impose capital punishment in the case of truly horrible crimes?

18

True Religion according to James

Read James 1:27–2:7

In the Epistle of James, a very Jewish Christian scripture, we read one famous bit of pragmatism that is quite opinionated about the fruits that genuine religion, whether that of authorities or that of common folk, should produce: "Religion that is pure and undefiled before God and the Father is this: to visit orphans and widows in their affliction, and to keep oneself unstained from the world" (1:27). James, of course, is the writing of the New Testament that most directly balances (some would say contradicts) the sort of supremacy that Paul gives to faith over works. I myself do not think that Paul and James cannot be reconciled, for mainstream Christianity has always tried to say two things at the same time: (1) everything pertaining to a right relationship with God is ultimately God's gift, and (2) unless we act out our professed love of God and reliance upon God, our profession is highly dubious. Here James might be paraphrased as saying: "Only when what we profess becomes practical and gets down to cases, can we say that faith is showing itself to be what the God of our Lord Jesus Christ expects and approves."

The first part of James's injunction, to visit orphans and widows in their affliction, could, of course, be taken minimalistically. That is, one could misinterpret it to mean that paying a few house calls and digging into one's pocket fulfill the ethical program incumbent on a Christian. The better interpretation, I am sure, takes widows and orphans as representatives of all the poor, suffering people who tend to languish on society's margins. In the example and preaching of Jesus, an effective sympathy for all such people is the only way to fulfill the Law and the prophets. Not to make the kingdom of God coincide with good news for such people— practical relief, as well as words of consolation and promise— is to twist the way that Jesus spoke and lived. The long line of saints who have spent themselves in charitable works, as well as the full programs of social relief that Christianity has sponsored, testify to the seriousness with which Christians have taken the injunctions of both Jesus and James. In our own day, the vigor with which many Christians have criticized governments that seem careless of the plight of the poor is keeping this prophetic heritage healthy.

We shall come to the second part of James's description of pure religion momentarily. Here we might profitably reflect on orphans and widows in particular. In many ancient societies, the widow was almost a stock figure of tragedy because marriage to a healthy man was a woman's major way to protection and support. Relations between tribal families more often than not were what anthropologists call "patrilocal," meaning that a woman moved into her husband's family circle. The view of what ought to happen to a woman when her husband died varied from culture to culture, but in some cultures a widow was considered an outright burden. Indeed, in classical Hindu culture, a woman whose husband died prematurely (a quite variable judgment) easily was considered to have caused his death by her bad karma. No doubt such a judgment made it easier for classical India to sanction *sati:* the burning of a widow on her husband's funeral pyre.

In the ancient Near East, no doctrine of karma determined a widow's fate so harshly, but clan relations and the generally patriarchal cast of the culture still conspired to make the widow's lot potentially grim. Her only hope was to have begotten healthy and successful children, above all vigorous sons, who then could pick up her husband's provision for her without a break in rhythm. On the whole, a woman had little chance of being an independent or self-sufficient agent. She was almost bound to be dependent on some male structure, and if that structure were not familial or kindly, she could have a miserable life. James expresses the direct ties that

refined Jewish religion made between caring for such unfortunates as a vulnerable widow and pleasing God in heaven.
One perhaps could say that not to be concerned for downcast
people such as many widows was to forfeit one's right to
mercy and help from God.

Much the same could be said about orphans, although of
course their plight was if anything worse. Children always
depended on their parents for just about everything, from
food and shelter to love and basic instruction. The orphan
may eventually come to special sensitivities and wisdoms, as
seems to have been the case with Muhammad, but being
bereft of one's parents is a bad formula for raising saints or
even solid citizens. On the whole it does more for criminality
than it does for genuine religion. The evangelists portray
Jesus as especially drawn to children, so James makes a valid
illation in supposing that Jesus' followers should show special
concern for children who have lost their main resource in life.
The use of the word *Father* for God but reinforces this line of
thinking. If we are to consider the divinity parental (perhaps
the word that best defuses the sexist possibilities in an
exclusively masculine designation) so that we can approach
God with the confidence of a child who asks for bread or
good advice, we ought to take special compassion on all
children, especially those whom fate has treated most harshly.
One starts to say that this is not difficult because tenderheartedness toward children seems so natural an inclination,
until all the pictures of children who have been abused or
abducted or even murdered flash before one's inner eye. Then
it becomes distressingly clear that, even in the supposedly
civilized twentieth-century United States, children need all
the protectors they can get.

The second part of James's description of religion, which
says we must keep ourselves unstained from the world,
depends on the negative strain of the Bible's ambiguous view
of "the world." Where the biblical doctrines of creation and
incarnation quickly mount a case for the goodness of the
world, the interpretation of sinfulness that we find in many
parts of scripture causes "the world" to stand for fallen
humanity in opposition to God. "The world," in this emphasis, is in general terms what "the flesh" is for the individual
person. As "the flesh" drags the personality away from God

(while "the spirit" draws the personality up to God), so "the world" summarizes much of the inertia that godlessness has built up. Since James is not writing with a Greek mentality and so does not think of either the flesh or the world as simply material (any more than he thinks of the spirit as immaterial), we should not infer that he wants us to flee from social activities or politics or artistic culture. To be sure, he does not evidence a personality that would spend much time on these things, but neither does he show himself to be a Gnostic or a Manichean—a heretic who would deny the significance of Jesus' real incarnation. Rather James is concerned that we make the Father of Lights, from whom every good gift descends, our primary treasure and not fall captive to mammon. He is concerned, in other words, that we not be practical idolaters.

If we link this conclusion with the prior focus on active help for widows and orphans, we suggest an interesting connection. True religion so translates love of God and love of neighbor that only the worldly (in the pejorative sense) get so stained or blinded that they do not make helping the unfortunate members of their society a very high item on the religious agenda. Conversely, practical idolatry or ignorance of God shows in people's unconcern for such suffering people as orphans and widows. All rhetoric to the side, if people are unwilling to spend the money and the energy necessary to alleviate the sufferings of the poor and abandoned, they have in them little reliable love of God. A church or a government or an individual may be judged by how it responds to the most vulnerable people in its midst. If a church, for instance, does little for widows in particular or discriminates against women in general, it fails the Jamesian test. If a government proposes tax reforms or establishes budgetary priorities that neglect the plight of its most needy citizens, it doesn't have much claim to the title "Christian" or "religious."

Why should James have focused on widows and orphans? How do the evangelists portray Jesus' interactions with children and women?

What obligations does a government have toward especially unfortunate or needy people in its population?

19

The Beastly Empire Envisioned by Revelation

Read Revelation 13:1-18

From chapter 11 of Revelation on, John of Patmos depicts the forces that oppose God and the church as savage beasts. Chapter 13 is interpreted by most commentators as representing the Roman Empire as *the* beast—the foremost foe of God then being used by Satan. In the background stands imagery from Daniel 7. In the foreground is the early Christian experience of trial under Roman rule.

The central irritant in relations between Christians and Roman culture was the idolatry, as Christians saw it, of the imperial cult associated with the emperor. To the Christian mind, the homage paid to the emperor and the confession of the emperor's divinity that (at least in principle) were required of all Roman citizens were but a species of commitment to Satan (whom Revelation symbolizes as the dragon):

> Men worshiped the dragon, for he had given his authority to the beast, and they worshiped the beast, saying, "Who is like the beast, and who can fight against it?"
> And the beast was given a mouth uttering haughty and blasphemous words, and it was allowed to exercise authority for forty-two months; it opened its mouth to utter blasphemies against God, blaspheming his name and his dwelling, that is, those who dwell in heaven. Also it was allowed to make war on the saints and to conquer them.
>
> —vv. 4–7

To do justice to even this short passage, let alone to all the imagery by which Revelation depicts opposition to God, would require much more space than we have available, so we must content ourselves with the most important observations. First, Revelation is through and through a highly symbolic work that very self-consciously draws on the conventions of Jewish apocalyptic. That literary genre interprets present history in terms of a supposed disclosure from God about the way that God is going to vindicate Christian followers against their oppressors. The quickest way to misinterpret any apocalyptic work, including Revelation, is to take its symbolism literally and think that the author received from heaven a sort of filmstrip of how the future would unfold. As scholars quickly learn when they trace down the symbols that John of Patmos uses, Revelation assumes a good familiarity with the Old Testament and recasts the apocalyptic tradition in terms of the conviction basic to Christianity that Jesus was resurrected by the Father.

Scholars debate the extent to which Christians in Asia Minor were suffering direct persecution from Rome. More recent opinion suggests that a general frustration over the mismatch between Christians' sense that the decisive victory had been won and their lack of power or material success in the culture at large was more significant. In other words, Revelation is as much an expression of the sense of alienation or not-at-homeness that Christian faith feels in most times and places as it is a protest against specifically Roman abuses.

Second, this way of looking at Revelation in fact makes it much more useful to us today than any literal tying of the text to horrors perpetrated by Nero or one of the other Roman emperors of the period would. The author is saying that God and mammon are always at war, and that, if anything, the victory of Christ has intensified the conflict. At the least, the resurrection of Christ and sending of the Spirit have shown Christians how much richer human potential is than what a purely materialistic or this-worldly horizon would allow. In Pauline terms, the body of Christ that people can constitute in the wake of the resurrection and gift of the Spirit ought to suffer no domination at all: neither Greek (or pagan) over

Jew, nor freeman over slave, nor male over female (Gal.
3:28). The stronger clash between Christian faith and secular
culture tends to occur when a given secular regime perceives
that Christian faith is critical of it on many scores. The Jews
had frequently aroused resentment in the Hellenistic and
Roman orbits because of their strict monotheism and their
lofty ethical ideals. The early Christians struck their pagan
neighbors as but Jews with a twist that gave them a special
zeal.

This opposition flared up in the centuries that followed
after Revelation, although the fact that Christianity became
the established religion of the Holy Roman Empire complicated matters considerably. With the demise of Christendom
in modern times, the antagonism has revived, as the antireligious
dimensions of two of the great modern revolutions, the
French Revelution of 1789 and the Russian Revolution of
1917, suggest. In the modern history of the United States,
things continued more the way they were through the centuries of Christendom, although under the surface mammon
was always putting the knife to faith. Today the most pernicious problems of American culture stem less from the
outright oppositon of atheists and believers than from the
pseudo-Christianity being put forward to support many policies, both economic and military, that directly contravene the
gospel.

For example, where the gospel puts God on the side of the
poor and beatifies those who are most distanced from mammon, our governmental policies and popular culture have
more respect for the rich. Where the gospel would engage in
spiritual struggles to ensure a regime of peace, justice, and
joy, our governmental policies and popular culture by and
large ignore spiritual forces—religious contemplation, creative humanistic study—and resort to money or military
might. The result is that today, as in the time of John of
Patmos, the people most led by Christ's spirit rise up in
prophetic oppostion to their secular leaders and pundits.

Let us return to our text, seeing whether the possibility of
quite contemporary implications won't bring some of the
phrases and figures more alive. In 13:4 we note that humanity is said to worship the dragon because he has given his

authority to the beast. The implication is that people in effect, if not in outright intention, give themselves over to evil because the allure of the worldly powers that be has dazzled them. Insofar as a secular power is unjust or ungodly, we might say, it represents Satan, who in turn is the great symbol for oppostion to, even hatred of, God. If God is light in whom there is no darkness at all, then Satan and evil are the darkness of lies, confusions, and misrepresentations. Doing ungodly work, many governments today fudge the facts, misrepresent their actions, corrupt language, and at times tell outright lies. The result is a twistedness of outlook that would be almost comically insane were it not so perverse and destructive. We call weapons that can destroy the earth "peacekeepers." We think that "mutual assured destruction" is a proper sort of deterrence from war. We abort "the products of conception" rather than babies or human fetuses. Our figures on unemployment, like our figures on casualties from the war in Vietnam, seem falsified.

The reason we ordinary citizens put up with this sort of darkness, verses 4-6 suggest, is that we are overwhelmed by the power of mammon and those who run its systems. We have so little interiority, so frail an appreciation of the aweful majesty of God, that we think those who can kill our bodies or wreck our bank accounts must be kowtowed to night and day. It is true that such people seem to have been given power to afflict all the saints (the passive voice of the verbs in Revelation 13:4-7 suggests that the author very much feels that all things are kept in the hands of God), but their reign, when measured against God's eternity, is almost ludicrously brief. If, for example, you go to the Roman Colosseum today, you find mainly a weary pile of stones. Whatever grandeur attended the spectacles there two thousand years ago is severely reduced by the smog.

Revelation takes aim at heaven, the realm where God clearly reigns. Compared to this realm, the achievements of mammon and evil are quite passing. With no fear of contradiction, then, Christians should raise their sights and take their orientation from the powers that cannot fail: justice and truth, love and compassion. Then, rooted in these, we may judge our present times crisply and helpfully. This immedi-

ately pulls out most of the beast's claws, and it gives a body
blow to the dragon. When we care only for the success that
Christ will endorse, we become Christian subversives.

---

*What are the main arguments for reading Revelation
symbolically?*

*Why is a Christian almost bound to be somewhat alienated
from secular culture?*

*What do you find to be the most beastly features of the
current culture of the United States?*

20

The Confession of Mark's Centurion

Read Mark 15:21-39

Mark 15 is a high point, if not the climax, of the drama that the author has constructed. There we see the end to which Jesus, the suffering Messiah, finally came. There the success that God most endorsed hangs bloodied as a Jewish subversive. Jesus cries out with the opening words of Psalm 22, "My God, my God, why hast thou forsaken me?" Some of the bystanders think he is calling upon Elijah, while another offers him vinegar to relieve his anguish. Mark describes Jesus' death most concisely, and then quickly gives us two interpretations of its significance: "Jesus uttered a loud cry, and breathed his last. And the curtain of the temple was torn in two, from top to bottom. And when the centurion [the Roman soldier], who stood facing him, saw that he thus breathed his last, he said, 'Truly this man was the Son of God' " (vv. 37-39).

The cry of Jesus is Mark's final way of emphasizing the suffering that God's bringer-of-salvation had to undergo. Since for Mark genuine Christian discipleship pivots on being willing to accept and imitate a suffering Messiah, the emphasis is meant to discredit any interpretation of Jesus or Christian faith that we might classify as "cheap grace." "If you want to follow Jesus," Mark in effect says, "you'd best keep before you the path that Jesus actually trod. Unless you take up your own cross, you can't be a genuine disciple."

The first interpretation of Jesus' death that Mark offers the reader occurs in the tearing of the curtain of the temple from

105

top to bottom. This symbolism suggests several things simultaneously. First, it suggests that believers in Jesus now have direct access to the holy of holies, which the curtain or veil of the temple had blocked off. In other words, through Jesus' death God has drawn near, the kingdom has come to be in human beings' midst. Second, the symbolism suggests that the religious order that centered on the temple and its sacrifices has been superseded.

Christians took perhaps fifty years to work out their interpretation of their relationship to Judaism, but when it became clear that most Jews were not willing to accept Jesus as the Messiah, Christians came to judge the religion of the temple passé. This judgment has often neglected the ongoing value of Jewish religion that Paul reflects upon in Romans 9-11, but how central it has become in Christian faith is suggested by such language as "the New Testament" and the "the new convenant." Newness, of course, need not signify improvement pure and simple. On the whole, though, Christians have thought that Jesus so fulfilled Jewish prophecy that with his death and resurrection a more gracious era dawned. As John 1:17-18 summarized this opinion: "The law was given through Moses; grace and truth came through Jesus Christ. No one has ever seen God, the only Son, who is in the bosom of the Father, he has made him known."

The second interpretation of Jesus' death that Mark 15 immediately gives us comes from the mouth of the centurion, whom we may take as the representative of fair-minded humanity at large. To Mark's mind, Jesus' fellow citizens have treated him both dishonestly and unjustly, being unwilling to recognize and accept the prophecy or grace in his message and person. The Roman centurion, who presumably has no special stake in the affair and is simply carrying out the order of higher-ups, is so moved by the spectacle that he bursts out with what, to Mark's mind, is the whole secret of Jesus' mystery. (Mark is the evangelist who most shrouds the mission and identity of Jesus in mystery.)

In the Hellenistic culture of the day, calling a man a "son of God" did not necessarily imply a claim to strict divinity. The phrase could mean much what we mean by the term *saint*. But the translators of the Revised Standard Version of the Bible rightly discern that Mark means something more profound and challenging, so they capitalize "Son." By the time that Mark was put into final written form, the theology of Paul and other schools of Christian reflection had found the significance of Jesus to break the boundaries of what a mere human being could have accomplished or been. So they were speaking in terms that implied Jesus' strict divinity—the implication that we may fairly find in this confession of Mark's centurion. Two and a half centuries later, when the church was debating the question of exactly how to phrase Jesus' status, the side that came to be considered orthodox was the one that said Jesus (the Logos) is consubstantial with God the Father: strictly divine.

This is our last biblical reflection, so perhaps it is especially appropriate for us to end at the center of the Christian "scandal." Jesus, the exemplar of Christian faith, dies on the cross as an accursed criminal. In the eyes of the Jewish law, he stands rejected by God. But in this depth of defeat or supposed rejection by God, his followers come to see the beginnings of a new creation. Their main warrant for this interpretation is the resurrection, which Mark only details in chapter 16. The resurrection, in fact, has always been the basis for the final Christian interpretation of the significance of Jesus' life and death. Focusing for the moment just on the cross, however, we can understand how affronted both Jews and pagans were by Christians' claims. To say that divinity would come into the world and take such a form of suffering and defeat turns ordinary human reason on its head. So Jesus is indeed a scandal or a stumbling block to those without faith, and a life based on Jesus should be similarly scandalous.

There are good reasons why people botch the meaning of the crucifixion, of course, and the maturity of faith that it takes to get the crucifixion right does not come with just a dab of water and a slick of oil. In itself, suffering is to be abhorred—our bodily pains are signs that something is very wrong. In itself, rejection by one's people and punishment as a criminal are indeed a very bitter defeat. So we cannot take our children into our churches, point at the crucified Christ, and assume that all will be obvious. As well, we should let the aversion from the crucifix that many refined people,

especially many refined Jews, feel remind us of the proper
mystery in our central symbolism. Jews of goodwill are not
recoiling from the crucifix or the cross simply because for
many centuries it has been the banner under which the most
poisonous anti-Semitism has paraded. (Think of the burning
crosses of the Ku Klux Klan.) They are also protesting the
interpretation of religion or of richest humanity that says it
must end in murder and blood.

Now, our response to these quite reasonable objections says
a lot about how we think a Christian program for peace and
justice should be founded, so we must make our response
carefully. First, the critics are right in saying that richest
humanity should not end in murder and blood—as far as they
go. The ''necessity'' that dogged Jesus and finally brought
him to the cross was the plan of a quite inscrutably good
God. For all the evangelists, the rejections that Jesus received
were in themselves wrong and sinful. But, the evangelists
quite rightly refuse to blame the victim for the wrongdoing of
the enemies who tried to wreck him. The cross is not a
judgment on the folly of Jesus so much as it is a judgment on
the evil of the people—representatives of us all—who strung
Jesus up. The ''folly'' of Jesus, moreover, was simply his
excess (by comparison with the rest of us) of love. In this he
represented very well the ''excessive'' God he called ''Father,'' for only a God much better than we can imagine (a
God who quite destroys the facile view of many atheists that
in making gods, human beings simply project themselves
onto a bigger screen) would bother to create human beings in
the first place, let alone bother to send his only begotten son
to rescue them when they had done their best to ruin
themselves.

So, the resurrection that changes the Christian drama from
tragedy to comedy (in the high sense of a resolution that
gives the human spirit hope) is ''fitting'' only on the deepest
level. Nothing in the death or resurrection of Jesus is ordinary or commonplace. Nothing in it is owed to us. That is the
reason that Christians from New Testament times have insisted
on the gratuity of salvation: the goodness of God far exceeds
what small, twisted human beings are competent to judge. As
a result, the basis for the best Christian programs for peace

and justice settles at the depths of the divine goodness. We have to try to make a world worthy of such a God, and we have to try to do it in ways that honor how God's own revealer and savior did his work. The Spirit of God who moves in all human beings' hearts is the one who can make social action on the model of Christ "reasonable." The movement of the Spirit is the best way for us to conceive how the possibilities of "humanity" can open up, so that people do not avoid the worst of human problems—radical injustice and slaughter—but also do not despair and write such problems into the marrow of what it means to be human.

No, on the Christian view of human nature the evils of injustice and warfare truly should not be. Yet they are, because of the irrational, ununderstandable reality of sin, and so we must contend with them. The great mercy of God is that Christ did contend with them, fully successfully, so that now we can contend with them (with solid hopes for success). The traditional hymn puts it all together very simply: "Dying he destroyed our death, rising he restored our life." That is the faith we need if we are to be peacemakers and apostles of God's justice.

Why does Mark put one of his most important interpretations of Jesus in the mouth of a Roman centurion?

Should Christians themselves feel scandalized by the cross?

What does the scene we have witnessed in Mark 15 suggest about the proper ways to go about our work for justice and peace?

III

WHAT, THEN, ARE WE TO DO?

21

The Relation of Prayer and Action

Read Luke 11:1-13

The centurion of Mark 15 could have been a model for the traditional Christian form of prayer known as "the application of the senses." In this form of prayer one would try imaginatively to watch, hear, touch, and even smell and taste the reality of a biblical scene. The centurion is presented as an eyewitness to the crucifixion. No doubt he heard the groans of anguish and the murmurings of the crowd. He may have touched the body of Christ when it was lowered from the cross. The smells he remembered and the taste left in his mouth probably were quite disagreeable, yet they too would have helped him, years later, to recollect the moving event. In the actual experience, as Mark presents it, the centurion observed and then expressed himself eloquently: "Truly this man was the Son of God!" If a Christian master of prayer were to consider the centurion a disciple, he or she certainly would be pleased with the honesty and realism he evidences. He observed what happened and was open to the deeper, religious significance. What his senses reported passed through his brain without distortion and so moved his heart appropriately. The judgment he made seems rightly welded to a choice in favor of Jesus. So the centurion leaves the scene of Mark's Gospel having impressed the reader that honesty had taken him to the side of the angels.

The further question that a master of prayer would want to raise focuses on the centurion's later actions. Did he, in fact, follow through on his experience, understanding, judgment,

and decision in favor of Jesus? Did his subsequent life bear
the imprint of the grace he had received and show the fruits
of faith, hope, and charity that Jesus himself would have
wished? After all, a man who has laid down his life for his
friends will be little gratified to have those friends stop at
admiration. He will want them to pass on to imitation, so that
they go and in their proper measures do likewise. The crux of
the centurion's response to what he witnesed was the fruits
that his later life showed. So is it with all the rest of us. The
quality of our prayer and the depth of our faith have an
intimately reciprocal relation with our behavior.

In using this somewhat inflated term *intimately reciprocal
relation,* I am trying to suggest that prayer and action
influence one another subtly and comprehensively. We don't
just fall on our knees, speak to God or try to take in a
scripture, and then rush off to act out what we have received.
We come to prayer shaped and bruised by our work and
social experiences. The questions we put to God and the
answers we find in scripture are greatly influenced by what
currently is going on in our lives. If we are in the midst of a
painful divorce, we will pray differently than we used to pray
in the easy early years. If we have just come from the birth of
a child, our posture will be different than it was after our
parent's funeral. True enough, God's word has an objectivity
that keeps it somewhat independent of our here-and-now
state. We may start with questions or emotions stemming
from anger and end up on a quite different plane of almost
wordless peace. Or we may begin like the Pharisee who stood
alongside the publican in the temple, thinking that we are
pleasing to God, only to leave considerably chastened. Nonetheless, our prayer will always be influenced by our current
situation.

It is true, of course, that the general interpretation of
Christian prayer that the masters lay before us insists that if
we go to prayer honestly we nearly always will leave consoled. Such "consolation" may become rather subtle in the
prayer of the mature, whom God can "test" in dark nights. In
their case, grace sometimes is just the strength to keep fighting
their discouragment at the revelations of their distance from
God that daily experience is bringing them. In most other

cases, however, it is the sign of the influence of "Satan" to find one's prayer (or even the prospect of going to prayer) discouraging. Even when we stand in the stench of fresh sin, the mystery of God invites us to come and be cleansed. Seventy times seven, we must learn that sin injures ourselves and other people far more than it injures God. Especially in the area where "sin" overlaps foibles and offenses against local mores (too large an area in many consciences; many people worry as much about offending the taste of their neighbors as they worry about violating the goodness of God), we have to get beyond our tidiness or untidiness of soul so that we can deal with the real business of loving God from the core.

Leaving prayer, we no doubt set out to enact the faith that has been renewed. People whose prayer is mainly meditative—turning over the truths of scripture or doctrine—probably tend to do this rather explicitly. People whose prayer consists more in gazing at a biblical scene or a crucifix, or in just trying to slip through a mass of distractions and rest wordlessly, imagelessly, in the dark depths of God, probably leave prayer with less explicit directives. Their ethical overflow or praxis is more holistic: trying to express everywhere (but especially in their love and their work, the two key hungers of the personality) the renewed perspective and refired warmth that the Spirit has given them.

Out in the world, people of prayer get a good testing that often turns them wry. What was clear and simple in the chapel seems muddied and slippery outside. What first seemed to be mainly a matter of courage can later be seen to be more a matter of prudence. For, not only is there the right thing to do, there is also the right time to do it. Indeed, there is the right posture in which to do it and the right tone in which to say it. All of this takes time to learn, even when one is naturally gifted with tact and has put in many hours on the prayer bench. But all of it is blessedly realistic and whole, making the roundness of Christian life, the constant circling from prayer to action to prayer to action, carry more and more valuable freight.

The simplest regime that one can discern, when one asks the different cultures how they have tried to move people forward into wisdom, is a circle rounding out a flow between poles of action or experience and reflection or prayer. We all only learn by experience. None of us is born wise (the wise countenance of many babies is one of nature's most intriguing little flirtations). So we all have to stumble ahead as best we can, making our way from point *a,* where we presently stand, to point *b,* which looms as the next landing spot. The difference between those of us who mature toward wisdom and those who remain immature overlong usually is the difference between the examined life and the life of those who won't reflect. The first challenge, then, is to become a reflective person: someone who takes a sabbath or a daily hour of quiet to drop the bustle and center down.

The second challenge (occasionally one finds a quietistic personality, for whom it is the first challenge) usually is not to get paralyzed by one's reflection. Only occasionally does this become the full-fledged paralysis that the spiritual masters sometimes refer to as *abulia* (the inability to come to a decision or plan [*boule*]). More frequently it takes the form of *acedia*: a general lethargy that is subtly underwritten by a doubt that one's actions can make any difference (either in the world at large or in the task of improving one's own personality). *Acedia* is a rather classical temptation (the desert fathers are always having to deal with it in their monks), and if you are suffering it, you may find some consolation in the thought that it means you have had enough experience of life to realize that effective grace (real signs of redemptive progress) indeed does not come cheaply. For your penance, though, I offer you the further traditional thought that *acedia* tends to signal a preoccupation with the self and its moods. The better preoccupation, of course, is with the divine mystery and the neediness of one's neighbors. So the time should soon come—verily, may well be at hand—when you let go of your self and get on with more important matters. Were this a book about prayer, we could begin to detail some of the things this suggests about prayer (mainly: the gentle movement through distractions and one's own troubles or moods down to the dark mystery of God [or out to a picture of the crucified], where one should just attend or abide holistically). Since this instead is a book about peace and justice with an accent on the active work that promotes them, the things we shall turn to are what a spirit-filled prayer might be urging us to do.

Compose a brief exercise in "the application of the senses," trying to bring alive for yourself what the Roman centurion might have experienced.

What is the rhythm between prayer and action that seems to you most simple and desirable?

What are the main obstacles that keep people from establishing this rhythm in their lives?

22

Possibilities on the Job

Read 2 Thessalonians 3:1-18

Work is one of the two central needs of the human personality. We may assume, therefore, that the spirit of Christ is urging us to square this so important dimension of our lives with the quiet imperatives of the gospel. First, the Spirit no doubt would like a say in what work we choose as the framework for our laborious creativity. Second, there are questions we may usefully raise about the possibilities for forwarding peace and justice that just about any job offers us.

On the first point, the Spirit probably is well conceived today as fighting to retrieve the traditional notion that work is a vocation. A vocation is a "calling" from God—the drawing or allure that one can discover by a steady examination of conscience. Several things conspire to make this notion less influential today than it was a few generations ago. For example, the increased pace of daily life and especially the influx of relatively trivial information, pressure most people toward a greater extroversion than one tended to find in the culture at large a few generations ago. A slow-paced culture, of course, certainly is no guarantee that people will be more thoughtful and reflective. Without good stimuli, it is true, people tend not to develop art or science or religion that is fresh and deep. But stimuli alone manifestly are not enough. As the poet Wordsworth might have put it at this juncture, only thoughts and emotions that have been recollected in tranquillity are like to bring us poetry and wisdom. So, if we are to retrieve the very useful notion that God

118

wants a say in what we choose as our life's work, we will need to fight the superficiality of our popular culture and drop out regularly for reflection.

We will also need to fight the notion that work is a purely secular affair—a matter of the six days that we can give to worldly matters, if not mammon, rather than a matter of the seventh day that we call the Sabbath. The notion in the United States that there is a proper separation of church and state is fine within its designated legal domain. Outside that domain, however, it tends to exert a pernicious influence, inclining people to think that work and politics and arts ought to stand apart from religion. That has never been the case in the great cultures that have shaped human history. Neither India nor China, neither Christendom nor the golden age of Islam allowed such a divorce between ultimate beliefs and daily work. The benefits that we associate with "modernity" (freedom of conscience, a proper criticism of religious superstition, and so forth) are great indeed, but sometimes we fail to note the liabilities. It is very hard, for instance, to have a profound culture when "pluralism" is interpreted as meaning that one has to keep the stance one takes toward the profound mystery of life separate from the positions one takes on economics or educational policy, on the arts or medical ethics.

Granted a willingness to fight for a more integral self and culture, however, today's Christian interested in peace and justice easily can consider the question of career or life's work as a decision that it is most fitting, indeed most necessary, to bring before God in prayer. For instance, granted a relatively equal aptitude for a career in business and a career in teaching, what does faith suggest about one's options? Well, faith certainly does not say that one cannot serve God in a business career, but it does call to mind those rather sobering sayings of scripture about the camel and the eye of the needle, about money and the root of all evils. Similarly, faith does not say that trying to bring young minds to maturity is the work befitting all laborers in the vineyard, but it does suggest that the young are a very important portion of the neighborhood that we are challenged to love as ourselves.

It is no secret nowadays that American education, both

lower and higher, is in deep trouble. One has only to go to the supermarket to find that the average high school graduate cannot even handle fractions. Some fast-food restaurants that offer opportunities for young workers take away the problem of computation on the cash registers. Instead of adding and subtracting, the employees have only to punch a picture of a hamburger or a small fries. It is a real if modest ministry, therefore, to join the little troop of those who would give their lives to trying to overcome this deculturation into which we've allowed the past generation to wander. And, despite the judgments of most state legislators, it is no easy line of work. In Christian perspective, the low wages that educators presently are forced to accept makes teaching a ministry performed at considerable personal cost. That so many young people, especially so many young women, continue seriously to consider it is an impressive testimony to the continuing action of the Holy Spirit.

I have not chosen to speak of education because it is the only option that puts the battles between God and mammon clearly. With more space at our disposal we could discuss medicine, the formal ministry, government service, the military, and many other areas to which people might be drawn for lofty, faith-filled reasons. The point in all such considerations would be to match who one is (the self and talents one has when most honest) with one's different options for work. These options, in Christian perspective, have to be weighed in terms of more than just their potential income and likelihood of developing one's talents. They have to be weighed as well in terms of their potential for serving the needs of both society at large and the church in particular.

I myself am most impressed by people who are willing to put in the hard labor necessary to be accounted competent in an area such as medicine or social work and who then work in that area quite matter-of-factly. I think, for example, of two women who are full-time counselors or caseworkers in state agencies for social relief. Both were drawn to this work for idealistic reasons, and both have found it a rather depressing initiation in the extent to which our society, or at least many individuals in our society, fail the hopes unleashed by Jesus' kingdom of God. One of these women has been at this work for many years—enough so that she is now a supervisor. I have been impressed by how little she dramatizes what she does. She virtually never goes on about the family tragedies that are the stuff of her daily round. She wastes no time in speechifying about politicians and red tape. She goes to church on Sunday, serves her family night after night, and from seven to four each workday does what she can do to console the poor and help the suffering. The rest she leaves to God.

I would say that this woman seems to have made a fine vocational choice, putting herself where she can exercise her evangelical convictions without a lot of fuss and sputter. The rest of us may not be in jobs that so directly engage with the work for peace and justice, but we too can try to do our bit without a lot of fuss and sputter. We can try to be honest and to speak up for what seems just. We can refuse to hide when it comes time to speak against policies that pursue excessive profits and ride roughshod over people. Against the stream of workaholism, we can insist on making time for family life, recreation, and prayer. Against the equally potent stream of laziness and shirking, we can put in an honest day's work. Even if the talk around the office is vicious, we can bite our tongues and refuse to fuel the flames. Even if the work turns dreary, we can weigh our obligations to our children before throwing it over and marching out.

The witness that many Christians and others of good will give each day in these humble ways is probably the main reason that American work has not become totally a darkness. In my own orbit of education, for instance, I am greatly edified when I step back from the trivial irritations and take into account how many people are in fact spending themselves idealistically. I work with talent that without question could find itself earning twice as much in other situations. It stays in education, more often than not, out of dedication to the young, to the exploration of truth, and to qualities in personal living that the pell-mell pace of many business careers won't allow. Quite modestly, my colleagues are saying there is more to life than money and status. There are possibilities in their jobs, they are saying at least implicitly, that point them to God's "more."

Is the notion that one's work should be a vocation still viable today?

What are the main factors that one should consider in making a vocational choice?

Do some works, such as education and social work, actually more directly forward the struggle for peace and justice than others?

23

Educating Children about Peace and Justice

Read Philippians 2:1-11

If work proves, under analysis, to offer us many hard decisions and ripe opportunities concerning peace and justice, so does love, our even more central human need. Here let us consider the children who represent the richest fruits of human love. How may we, in our dealings with our children, express our love of life and God? How may we contribute to the prime evolutionary task, which is warding off death for another generation and making the world fit to live in?

Obviously enough, we may do this mainly through our example. The familiar saying, "I can't hear your words because your example is shouting," holds for children in spades. Long before they have grown able to understand the subtleties of our speech and instruction, our children have been imprinted by our example and overall personality. This simple fact of family life and child-rearing is scary, of course, for none of us is the person we'd like our children to become. All of us are nipped here and torn there in ways that we hope our children can avoid. On the other hand, children often are kinder than we think, and so, perhaps with the exception of during their teenage years, our children usually forgive us our foibles and failings. The only thing they cannot forgive us, in the name of simple truth, is a substantial dishonesty or lovelessness. Granted a substantial honesty and love, however, our children will more than muddle through. In the present context, then, we need only reflect on what honesty and love require if they are to move our children to an appreciation of the imperatives of justice and peace that we can harmonize with Christian faith.

A first matter is how just children find their home situation to be. By this I mean more than the important but quite elementary matter of whether or not parents render their own children justice—whether they listen to their children's point of view, apologize when they have been unduly harsh with their children, give their children room to make mistakes, and so forth. Rather, assuming this, I mean whether children find in the whole slant of their upbringing an advocacy of the poor, an awareness of the manifest injustices in our country and world, and a sense of responsibility to help lessen these evils. Negatively, one could say that children who grow up in a household that never discusses racism, sexism, the patterns of unemployment, or the dangers that mammon presents to the common good are being shortchanged. On the other hand, children who grow up in a household that is simply negative or cynical about these matters, inculcating the notion that things have ever been thus or that the downtrodden are down mainly through their own fault, is equally pernicious.

The only fully adequate upbringing in Christian perspective is one that takes the twofold commandment as a gentle yet constant pressure to hasten the day when the world will not be so flagrantly divided into haves and have-nots. The particulars of this upbringing, of course, will vary from household to household. One family may especially target resistance to militarism while another family may focus on economic imbalances. The starting point doesn't matter crucially, because the great problems of warfare and injustice today crisscross relentlessly. What does matter crucially is that there be a starting point and a process—that children grow up in households that make opposing injustice and working for peace as standard as sugar-free peanut butter.

Children will take most of their cues about sexual equality, racial equality, economic equality, and the like from the ways that Mom and Dad interact, treat people of other races, and deal with money. If there is not sexual equality under one's own roof, speaking about women's liberation or even about the degradation of rape will be somewhat like blowing smoke. If their parents have no friends from outside their own racial or ethnic bloc in a town offering many opportunities for such catholicity, children will have little personal sense of what "the melting pot" can and cannot mean. And if parents must overbuy and undersave, like the American middle class at large, children hardly can be expected to have a solid defense against mammon.

Sixty years ago, Monsignor John A. Ryan, a pioneer in the modernization of Christian social theory, gave out the ringing opinion that "the only life worth living is that in which one's cherished wants are few, simple and noble." That is the sort of opinion that Christian parents serious about bringing their children up with a hunger for peace and justice will be trying to exemplify and inculcate. The life that children see displayed on television and in the "Living" section of the Sunday newspaper on the whole is not worth living. It is idle, gilded, and self-serving. For what are fashion and fancy food compared to the possibilites of prayer and the desperate needs of the global poor? To cherish a penthouse with three large bedrooms and four and a half bathrooms, as a booklet of plans for condominiums recently encouraged me to do, is to show oneself a fool as well as a minion of mammon. A population fitting into three bedrooms could never keep four and a half bathrooms employed. That a small population should need such lavatory space to beautify rather than simply relieve itself merely says that our narcissism has spawned like cancer.

The noble life to which any people of wit want to raise their children rests on quite traditional and biblical judgments about the proper hierarchies of human choice. First, the spirit is more important than the body, although of course the body has very solid rights. Granted food and health, we should focus on the education that will refine the mind and on the twofold love, love of God through prayer and love of neighbor through self-sacrifice, that will fulfill the heart. All of Madison Avenue notwithstanding, high fashion and fastidious food will not make our children happy, let alone make them admirable. God has so saved us from Madison Avenue and all other purveyors of foolishness that we know, in the best parts of ourselves, that understanding and love are our crux. We have minds to nourish that are much more important than

our palates. We have work to do that far outweighs our need
for sport. Leisure, which deeper sociologists have long realized is the basis for culture, emphatically does not mean week-
ends given over to carnality and excess. Unemployment and
debt, as even the economists realize now and then, are most
significant for what they say about our diseases of soul.

What, then, is a parent to do? Mainly, a parent is to accept
soberly the fact that responsible Christian parenting today
must paddle against the mainstream. It must limit children's
exposure to television, rock music, and other potent sources
of spiritual rot. It must limit budgets for clothes and recreation. Positively, it must find ways for the family to do
something to protect the environment, build up the neighborhood, stay aware of the hordes of suffering people abroad,
and love only God unlimitedly. It must prove, by the daily
doing, that a simple set of noble wants is immensely richer
than a complicated, overstuffed life that lusts for glitter. A
parent must encourage not only education but also spiritual
development.

To be sure, this is far easier to dictate than it is to effect.
Children can protest that they have not freely signed on for
such a countercultural journey and that they only want to be
one of the crowd. But there are ways of honoring this protest,
many forms of compromise, that do not release either the
parents or the children from the central imperatives of the
gospel. There can be free hours and free dollars that children
can use as they wish, while the parents continue to determine
what basic, overall thrust of the family's lifestyle best squares
with the gospel. There can be special times of family sacrifice for the sake of peace or the poor. In the long run, parents
can only hope and pray that their children will come to
realize how much better off they are for having had firm
guidelines and high ideals. In the long run, the Spirit is the
one who bears the responsibility for making such correct
choices persuasive.

What are the wants on which a truly noble life will focus?
What is a balanced judgment on television and rock music?
How may parents who are trying to lead lives that build up
peace and justice console themselves?

24

Stewardship of the Local Land

Read Mark 6:30-44

Among the four primal realities that define our world (nature, society, the self, and divinity), nature has suffered the most neglect by Christian social thought. Where God, the self, and society have all received proper attention, nature has languished under rather slanted interpretations of Genesis that have helped Christians to use or even to abuse it as they saw fit. When human technology was rather limited, the devastations that we could wreak on nature were equally limited. Now that our technology has made us powerful polluters, nature is reeling close to the border of no return. A generation ago we started to realize that unless we changed our ecological ways, there would be only smog and acid rain on our children's horizons. Our general consciousness is better today, but still hardly what the dimensions of the ecological crisis demand. We do our children no favor, therefore, unless we show them from their earliest years that the only responsible attitude toward nature is one that makes us stewards of the local land.

"Stewardship" is something of a halfway house in environmentalist circles, being less than the democracy that thoroughgoing environmentalists would like but considerably more than the lordship over the land that has brought us into our present ecological straits. Thoroughgoing environmentalists often want to legislate for nature sovereign rights close to those enshrined in the U.S. Bill of Rights. Religious people can travel much of this pathway, too, because any religious person who has taken a doctrine of creation or monotheism to heart has confessed that God alone has full rights over nature. Where religious people of biblical inspiration tend to separate from thoroughgoing environmentalists is in denying that human beings are wholly level with the rest of creation. The notion that human beings have been made in the image of God, while the rest of creation are but vestiges of God, inclines religious people of biblical inspiration to speak up for a use of nature that will first benefit the human species. "Stewardship" therefore has come on the scene as a term that might designate a properly limited and responsible benefit from nature. When human beings are good stewards of creation, both they and creation at large will flourish. There will be room for development, but there will be a firm limit to the damages that developers will be allowed to do. There will be an appreciation of the achievements of technological research, even in areas of nuclear energy and chemical synthesis, but there will also be a firm will not to allow new technologies further to pollute our endangered ecosystems.

I am not going to rehearse the figures on how badly our ecosystems are in fact now endangered. Any primer in ecological science, and even my own little theological work *Ecology and Religion,* will furnish such information to those who want it. The deeper problem is that most of our population does not want it. The Northern nations have built a modern lifestyle on a technology that treats nature wantonly, so only those in the Northern nations who are willing to face the possibility of a radical conversion away from their modern lifestyle come to ecology books with eyes to see.

In recent years, to be sure, the consumption of energy has declined in the United States, so there should have been more space in which to begin to maneuver for better interactions with the globe's quite fragile holistic system. But the main engine of this decline has been economic rather than philosophical, so it rests on a precarious basis. For example, we have witnessed few signs of a new mentality that would make "environmental impact" more than another morass of legalism and bureaucratic frustration. Acid rain continues to fall, while the lawyers and government bureaucrats diddle. The greenhouse effect continues to grow. Our explorations in space have confirmed the impressions of all who have sensed that the global envelope of air has become significantly polluted: astronauts riding satellites can now see a dingy aura. Regularly we bemoan these facts yet consider only their economic or aesthetic implications. Regularly the nation professing to be one of the most religious in the world says virtually nothing about the religious implications of humanity's fouling its God-given nest.

The technology of modernity is, in simplest analysis, the source of one of humanity's primary temptations to think itself divine or at least independent of God. Laplace, the French scientist who claimed to have no need of the "hypothesis" of God to write his explanations of the heavens, was no technocrat, but he was a thorough modern. And, of course, modern technology succeeded so brilliantly in many of its undertakings that only recently (at the dawn of what some call postmodernity) has it become apparent that there is no more salvation in nuclear reactors or new hybrids of grain than there is in any other human manipulation of creation. Salvation only comes when human beings are given a more than human standpoint and power that works to make them whole. On their own, human beings tend to use even the best of their achievements in ways that express their sin as much as their grace. The best scientists and engineers now recognize this, so they do not look to science or engineering for their ethical directives. They know that we must decide what we will do with computer science and genetic engineering by holistic, overall standards that fall outside the scientific and technological horizons.

The Christian contribution to these decisions, as I see it, puts some strong hindrances in the way of technological development. (The development of pure science is a trickier question, best left for another occasion.) Technological development by its nature wants to intrude into the environment and reshape it. In the case of nuclear engineering, for example, it wants to release the energy of primal matter and set it at the service of the local community. Prescinding from the economic dimensions of this desire, which of course are massively influential, we can see the bedrock issue rather clearly. Should one so intrude into a local environment, even for the benefit of the human inhabitants of that environment, that one endangers its overall welfare significantly?

The prudent answer, I believe, is no, one should not so intrude. At least until one reaches a crisis situation in which the need for nuclear energy is truly pressing, one should not design and build nuclear power plants until one is able to guarantee their safety. In the case of nuclear energy, we will not have reached "safety" until we have a proven method of disposing of the radioactive wastes. Probably the only way we shall secure such a method will be through breakthroughs that allow us to mutate the radioactive materials into something not radioactive. For us to have spent the past generation erecting nuclear facilities, both those for energy and those for weapons, without such an ability to change the wastes has been imprudent and unethical in the extreme. We have, in fact, poisoned the earth, which continues to be the mother of us all, enough times to give any sane people great pause for shame and reflection. Instead of the lies of spokespersons who have assured us that "incident" after "incident" has been insignificant, we should have been hearing, from the pulpits throughout the land, insistent clamors for change.

Peace and justice will mean little if there is no earth that can support healthy human, animal, and vegetative life. An improved gross national product for the third world will be a dubious blessing if it but advances the pollution one finds in New Delhi and Bangkok. The simple yet noble life that we need worldwide requires in as many places as not a cutback on consumption and pollution. The have-nots who despise environmentalists who speak about the global dangers of pollution, accusing such environmentalists of merely wanting to perpetuate the current patterns of economic and political domination, make considerable psychological sense, but they make no ecological sense at all. Environmentalism is not just a little aesthetic enthusiasm of the fortunate who want to keep pure their ranches in the heavens. Environmentalism is the cause the earth itself asks us to promote if we are not to be the assassins of creation.

What rights ought Christian faith to accord to nature?

How badly polluted in fact are our interlocked systems of water, land, and air?

How much defense does Christian faith have in store for the modern technological way of life?

25

Peace and Justice between the Sexes

Read Galatians 3:23-4:7

The big hit of the 1984-85 television season was the "The Cosby Show," a situation comedy featuring a black professional couple and their five sprightly kids. Most of the kudos that this show received was well deserved, for the show was both very funny and very healthy. While I think the show has some limitations, here I want to use its warmth as a springboard to some reflections on how we might further peace and justice between the sexes. The show suggests that healthy, equal relations between mother and father have much to do with children's happiness and security. It portrays a marriage in which both woman and the man are their own persons. Yet it never makes their independence, or even their idiosyncrasies, outweigh their agreement to merge their selves for the good of their marriage and family life as a whole. The harmony and mutual sacrifice of their love, in fact, is the most persuasive basis for the happiness of their children. Even when the cheerleading gets a bit heavy and we feel manipulated by "positive" feelings of support and self-worth, we have to agree that these feelings are in sufficiently short supply in many households to justify the show's larding them on so generously.

The bottom line in a Christian view of the sexes, I believe, is Paul's sense that the new creation of the risen Lord has wiped away all basis for one dominating over the other. In the grace of Christ, man and woman are free to work out any combination of their similarities and differences that truly

honors their co-humanity and co-saintliness. Generally, therefore, one cannot say ahead of time that either "traditional"
or "liberated" ways of setting the heterosexual relationship
are to be preferred. Generally, the only thing one can say is
that each partner to a marriage should pull a fair-sized load and
receive a fair-sized set of rewards.

Those who find the historical record quite complicated and
who, therefore, refuse to judge the past to have been all
oppression of women by men have a lot of wisdom on their
side. In any relationship as holistic as the interaction of wife
and husband, simplistic equations are bound not to balance.
Women who seem to be powerless can wield great influence
by indirection. Men who seem nearly inarticulate and emo-
tionless can be the rock by which the family stands. Stereotypes do more harm than good when we take them for the
thing itself. Concretely, the thing itself is always unique: no
marriage exactly reproduces any other.

My own sense of the way forward toward great peace and
justice between the sexes plays in what I hope is a demilitarized
zone between stereotypes and the despair of making any
generalizations at all. First, I think that each couple ideally
should work out in considerable freedom its own sense of
"justice" and "peace." Whether their arrangement fits traditional or quite innovative patterns, the crux would be their
own free entry upon it. (This "freedom," to be sure, would
be constrained by economics, physical health, education, and
all the other factors that constrain any choice in the area of
work or friendship.) Second, granted this ground-level assumption, I think the likelihood is that more women than
men would find their "problem" to be integrating a natural
orientation to interrelationship with a need for greater self-
reliance. Conversely, I think the likelihood is that more men
than women would find their "problem" to be integrating a
natural orientation of self-reliance with a need for greater
interrelationship. These are rather commonsensical observations, of course, but I have found them supported by such
data-based or observation-based theories as those of Carol
Gilligan and Robert Kegan, both of whom have been laboring
to extend the influential work of Lawrence Kohlberg on the
development of moral intelligence.

To date, the men in our Western societies have been raised to a model or ideal of independence. Even when they fail to realize this ideal, as many men manifestly do, the sketch has been to become a person relatively self-sufficient. Women have been raised to find their sense of identity or self through relationships: with their spouses, their children, their friends. Even when women have failed to realize this ideal, it has pressured and prodded them. Neither model, in itself, is objectionable, as long as it has windows and collateral corridors. A man can seek to grow to be self-reliant, and if he seeks honestly and wisely, he will discover through this process itself how ''self-reliance'' must come to be qualified. For example, there is the bedrock reliance upon God that he must confess, on pain of being the psalmist's fool who says in his heart there is no God. There is the mutuality in his relationships with his friends, his children, and the person he would call bone of his bone. In such relationships, he should quickly come to see, there must be receiving as well as giving. Otherwise the love withers and with it most of the glow that makes life worth living.

From the woman's side, the model can be approached in much the same way. A woman can start with an orientation to ''be-with'' others, rather than with an orientation that paints her standing alone, and if she follows it faithfully enough, she will one day see that she cannot ''be-with'' her friends or her children or the one for whom she has left father and mother unless she is a person in her own right. Just as a man who can have no vulnerability or needs is a man who cannot fully honor some very simple truths, so a woman who must be a clinging vine is retarded and blocking some truths of conscience. We should go gently with both such underdeveloped people, of course, realizing that they probably but manifest more extremely deficiencies we ourselves possess. But we should also make sure that we learn from our observations what a fully mature personality, male or female, would be.

A fully mature personality, male or female, can be content in either solitude or togetherness. There is a time to be alone, and there is a domain of every life that no one but God can fully share, as death painfully dramatizes. There are many times, fortunately, when it is not good to be alone, for it is togetherness, rather than solitude, that has spawned most of the world's music, poetry, theater, religious ritual, medicine, exploration, and education. A woman who has spent the first twenty years of her marriage immersed in caring for her spouse and her children may need the second twenty years to be richer in opportunities to be alone. A man who has tried to blaze a trail to independent status and security through an immersion in work may at forty-five want to spend more time in intimate relationships of friendship, parenting, and spousal romance. If the two partners can share their feelings and senses of shift, they should be able to accommodate one another relatively gracefully. If one or both has become a prisoner of the model according to which he or she was supposed to develop, all involved in the marriage are bound to suffer.

The contemplative side of Christian life ought to help us stay in touch with our feelings and shifts and ease our way to expressing them. The call we feel to love our neighbors as ourselves ought to be a salutary pressure to listen to others and try to help them out. Occasionally two people will find their directions or senses of need conflicting, and then they will rightly feel put to the test. Neither one should feel that all right is on one person's side. Both should feel that the problem is "ours" rather than "mine" or "yours." Marriage is the adventure of trying to become one flesh. It is the human analogue of God's promise to Israel to share its time and reveal the divine identity progressively. We only develop who we are and show it forth, both to one another and to ourselves, progressively—over time. We all begin callow and must pray to God to end wise. Justice occurs between the sexes when their equal condemnation to journeying forth into the night makes them both compassionate. Peace and joy occur when their love helps them join arms against the bogies of the night and so radically diminish them.

What is the Christian foundation for equality between the sexes?

What is a proper personal independence?

How ought the relationships of friendship and family life to figure into our models of personal maturation?

26

The Dark Cloud of Nuclear War

Read Revelation 16:1-21

The entertainment industry to which we are regularly exposed often leaves out large parts of the reality that any truly responsible citizen must be prepared to face. On matters of economic justice, for example, the affluence of the doctor/lawyer in television series needs the complement of scenes with people who suffer in the lower tax brackets. But perhaps the biggest failing of American popular culture at large comes from its crashing silence about the nuclear arms race. Much of our difficulty in the contemporary U.S., in fact, comes from the way so many forces in our culture conspire to distract us from the single most fearsome peril threatening our world.

The entertainment industry is so bound to U.S. business at large, and U.S. business at large is so tied into military contracts, that the conspiracy against confronting our greatest peril is not at all surprising. Indeed, at the margins of the psychology of the issue of peace and war one can make a case that we do need distraction from time to time, lest the grim realities drain away all our humor and hope. But a culture, like an individual, is off center when it does not put first things first.

The first thing for an individual is loving God wholeheartedly and loving one's neighbor as oneself. The negative correlative of this first thing is doing one's best to overcome the idolatries that are the main impediments to obeying one's great commandments. The first thing for a culture at large is

137

exactly the same. The negative correlative for a culture at large therefore is doing its best to overcome the idolatries that impede its radical obedience to the call to love and sanity.

By most of the criteria that a religious conscience would muster, the nuclear arms race is United States citizens' greatest impediment to love and sanity. Unless we halt this arms race, taking away both the motives and the means that threaten a holocaust of creation, we have no secure future and so little present mental health. "Security," to be sure, is a word that calls for distinctions. None of us know the hour or the day of our death. All of us have to pray that the judge before whom we are sure to come will treat us mercifully. Yet we all ought, after so much evolutionary travail, to be able to plan on creation's continuing. We all ought to be able to beget children and tousle the hair of their children confident that the twenty-first century will give them a fair shake. The mystery of God will always remain richer than what we can descry. It is quite possible that that mystery will have to bring grace out of the horrible sin of a nuclear war. But for us not to work in the quite unmysterious intermediate zone of human politics so that nuclear war becomes virtually outlawed once and for all would be a terrible default of our responsibilities. Consequently, for us to abet the conspiracy of the forces that want to keep our eyes averted from the buildup of nuclear arms is to stain our consciences with their idolatry and atheism.

The dark cloud of nuclear war has become more than a symbolic figure. Increasingly, scientists are confident that the phenomenon of "nuclear winter," in which a nuclear cloud would effectively cut off all sunlight to parts of the earth, attends any significant explosion of nuclear power as a solid and serious risk. Were the sun indeed to be blocked out by the smoke and debris of nuclear explosions, the entire eco-system of the planet probably would suffer a lethal blow. The psychology of military strategists has become so perverse in some circles that many have resented the arrival of the data on the probabilities of nuclear winter. These data, some have said, complicate strategic policy, forcing those who plan the scenarios for our exploding nuclear bombs to deal with new and finally untestable hypotheses. Indeed, they raise the possibility that all of our previous theories of deterrence will soon become obsolete, since no country possessing large nuclear bombs will rationally be able to risk using them. But finally the force of the data has broken through the strategists' strong will not to know, making considerations of nuclear policy a whole new ball game.

When discussing peaceful nuclear energy, I proposed that the only truly ethical policy would be not to employ a technology until it had been proven thoroughly safe. In that case, the problem was the disposal of radioactive wastes, and the status report showed that the problem has not to date been solved. By the same principle, prudent ethicians have long warned against any use of large-scale nuclear weapons. What we can extrapolate from the experiences of Hiroshima and Nagasaki suggests that today's bombs would do unimaginable amounts of damage. Not only would the loss of human life in a sizable nuclear attack mount into the tens of millions, but the biosphere itself would certainly be imperiled. The phenomenon of nuclear winter but adds greater precision to this "tutiorist" position. (In ethical parlance, tutiorism [from the Latin word for "safer"] is the position that says we should follow the safer viewpoint. In the present case, it would be the view that we should not use nuclear energy until we have moral certainty that we will not do more harm than good.) What refined moral intelligence has long cried out—nuclear war would be a sacrilege—is now being confirmed by scientific intelligence.

The churches, to their great credit, have been in the vanguard of those offering citizens ways to protest the current policies of the nuclear powers, and people wanting to become active opponents of the arms race need only get in touch with the national, if not the local, board of just about any sizable denomination to find groups with whom they may collaborate. The marches, letters to representatives in Congress, support of educational programs, prayer vigils, and the rest may seem to have had little effect, but in fact they have created a climate of opinion in which the case of hard-line hawks typically is given less attention. We shall deal in the next section with the cornerstone of the hawkish case (the genuine threats from Communism), but here we may take comfort in the fact that nuclear weapons themselves have become in most circles symbols of obscenity. One would wish that this sort of obscenity, rather than the type that too many small-town vigilantes find in books like *The Catcher in the Rye,* would capture the country's imagination, but we must take what victories we can get. I myself count it a considerable victory that the majority of U.S. citizens now probably do think that their government's stated policy of nuclear buildup is crazy. The fact that, apart from some who think that God wants to use nuclear holocaust as means of taking us all up into the heavenly "rapture," people of faith are massively opposed to nuclear war and the preparations that make nuclear war ever more likely surely should console all who hunger for the Bible's shalom.

We will not blow away the dark cloud of nuclear war, of course, until we become more filled with the Holy Spirit than presently we are. The Spirit blows where it wills, to be sure, but it is impossible not to believe that the Spirit wants to blow nuclear holocaust off the horizon of possibility. The problem, then, is with neither God nor the stars. The problem is where it almost always is: with ourselves. We have to want peace and justice much more than presently we do. We have to be willing to smash the idols of wealth, ego, and pseudosecurity that currently dominate our national psyche. It is because we will not live in genuine faith, trusting the darkness of God, that we human beings have heaped up stores of nuclear weapons all over the world. It is because we cannot ask and give forgiveness that we are dizzied by this mad spiral. The winter of our discontent has not yet become icy enough to push us to a second spring of Easter faith. The phenomenon of nuclear winter is one more warning that the time is short and the peril is not likely to diminish.

How should humankind react to the phenomenon of "nuclear winter"?

Where does active opposition to the buildup of nuclear weapons now stand in your church?

How does the Christian doctrine of reconciliation bear on the grid-lock that has afflicted the superpowers?

27

A Christian Critique of United States Foreign Policy

Read 1 Corinthians 13:1-13

A good question to put to the foreign policy of any nation, in light of the massive threats entailed in nuclear war, is the extent to which that policy lessens the likelihood of nuclear war. It may do such lessening in various ways, of course, ranging from those that make the enemy pause before considering any attack to those that win the enemy over to friendship. The first sort of deterrents we might call negative and provisional. They mainly suggest to the enemy that war will have grievous consequences at home so long as the present balance of power is in place. The second sort of deterrents we might call positive and longer-lasting. They suggest to the enemy that a fund of good will can exist such that most differences or irritations can be negotiated. They also promote the notion that good relations should be the normal state of affairs, from which even disagreements, let alone wars, would be a sorry aberration.

In terms of dealing with the Soviet Union, it seems that the posture of the United States has waffled between these two positions. More years than not, unfortunately, we have inclined to the first position, viewing the Soviet Union as much less than a friend. Of course, there are many and good reasons for this position, especially if one stays at the level of secular analysis (making nothing of either sin or redemption). Still, from a Christian perspective, we must criticize a cold-war mentality and even more a hot-war mentality, as superficial and probably self-serving. These mentalities tend to depict the adversary as a caricature, exaggerating the evils of its regime. They tend to overlook or suppress the features in our own regime that give credence to the adversary's fears or accusations of evil-doing. The result in the case of Soviet-U.S. relations has been more ideological clash than straight-forward practical discussion and conflict-resolution.

The biblical rule, to which we have alluded several times, is that we should judge people mainly by their fruits—what they in fact do or don't do. We may listen to their words, but we should not let their words represent their whole reality. Their whole reality is much better represented by what they do. This criterion is a sharp sword, of course, and all of us have good reason to fear it. Applied to the Soviets, it brings into focus the many brutalities visited on their citizens since the revolution of 1917 and also the many places abroad where they have been trying to foment unrest and revolution. However, it also brings into focus the improvements that have come to the peoples of the Soviet republics, as well as the miseries afflicting many people in the foreign countries where the Soviets have been active. Applied to ourselves, the biblical criterion spotlights such generous undertakings as the opposition to Nazism in World War II and the Marshall Plan that helped Europe rebuild. Domestically, it spotlights the freedoms that our people enjoy and their overall cultural prosperity. Negatively, however, the biblical spotlight makes us recall the imperialism we visited on Vietnam, our support for many corrupt foreign regimes, and the injustices at home that blacks, poor people, and women especially have suffered. There is good and bad, therefore, on both countries' records.

I do not mean, by this parallelism, to say that I would just as soon live in the Soviet Union as in the United States. I think that, on the whole, our record and system stand better in the sight of divine justice. But I do mean to say that we have a solid basis for understanding why people might be attracted to communism or socialism. I do mean to say that our record, especially in the crucial matter of nuclear warfare, gives us solid reasons for reaching down to the humility that any successful resolution of conflicts requires. Since we are the people who detonated the only two nuclear weapons that to date actually have been used, we have a certain burden of proof in this area. The massive buildup of nuclear weapons by the Soviets is a terribly negative sign of their mentality, of course, but our own buildup has been nearly equally impressive.

The Christian critique of this linchpin of U.S. foreign policy, our attitude toward communism (as we see it lived out in the Soviet Union), therefore begins with some self-criticism. If communism has often shown itself to be a horrible ideology, capable of killing hordes of people without any sign of remorse, democratic capitalism has also shown itself to be pernicious, as both our militarism and the gap between rich people and poor people in our spheres of influence argue. We cannot honestly or realistically look at any other regime as though we were pure saints riding immaculate white horses. We have, at least implicitly, to see that our way is not the only way and that we still have some penances to perform.

This, I think, is the solid basis for many Christian activists' refusal to equate Americanism or capitalism with the gospel of Christ. The former is a quite fallible history and theory. The latter is a call for conversion day after day. And if this critical stance toward all ideologies pertains to the area of Soviet-U.S. relations, all the more does it pertain to the relations between the United States and the lesser powers. The rhetoric of some Latin Americans and Africans may be irritating, but under it we should hear not just the misinformation given them by Soviet agents but also the frustration caused by their grinding poverty. Insofar as we have supported Latin American regimes that seemed only to safeguard the rights and wealth of the upper classes, we rightly reap the anger of those who hate the sufferings of the majority. The same is true for an African regime such as that of Pretoria. Insofar as we have been slow to condemn apartheid and pressure the South Africans to repent of this racist system, we have quite legitimately been perceived as wanting only to maintain our own economic and racial advantages.

The Christian critique of U.S. foreign policy, as the Christian critique of any country's foreign policy, would have judgment begin at home. This is just the extension of the church's mandate from 1 Peter 4, to let judgment begin with the household of God. We in the United States have only limited control over what other countries can do. Our first imperative is to clean up our own act. Until we can square our foreign policy with the justice and peacemaking laid before us as the biblical demand, we have no right to call our country Christian. The tears we shed for the victims of oppression will seem crocodile tears and the prayers we pray will seem pharisaic. We need not throw prudence out the window, but we do need to throw out hypocrisy. Many of the policies that we pursue under the name of anti-Communism are in fact very self-serving and hypocritical. To prop up the dictator Somoza, for example, rather than trying to support the forces working for a more just Nicaragua, clearly put us on the wrong side. Instead of repenting of our evil, we have only compounded it by not dealing with the Sandinistas and helping them take the better paths that many of their leaders, such as the Cardenal brothers (both priests), certainly wanted.

The prudence that I mentioned also is implied in the biblical criterion of fruits. If the Sandinista government, or any idealistic group, in fact slaughters Indians and spews hatred indiscriminately, we hardly can anoint it. One has, in fact, to sympathize deeply with the professionals in our diplomatic corps, since so frequently there are very few "good guys" with whom they might build the better basis of friendship. It is understandable, therefore, that they and people in the CIA should become hard-liners and paranoid. But understanding this hardly justifies trying to make it the Christian perspective, as one finds some religiously motivated hard-liners seeming to do. The doctrine of holy war, which is the ultimate action to which the notion of acting violently in order to wipe out evil reaches, becomes outmoded and barbaric when one stands by the cross of Jesus Christ. We see this when Shiite Islam goes crazy and throws away millions of lives. We fail to see it in the actions and topsy-turvey rhetoric by which too many in this country try to justify the buildup of nuclear arms, in our own fomenting of insurrections, or in our own preparations for invading Latin American countries. So if today we would hear God's voice, we would find great reason to unharden our hearts and change our foreign policy.

————————————————

Is it valid to say that Christian convictions cannot realistically be applied to Soviet-U.S. relations?

Is it appropriate to speak of a need for conversion and penance in the United States and to think that appreciating this need could remove some of our psychological intransigence?

What is a valid fear of communism, in the context of relations with Latin American countries?

28

Voting with One's Ballot, One's Money, and One's Feet

Read Mark 12:1-17

I have been stressing ways of looking at the foundations and central obstacles that structure the task of achieving peace and justice. In these last meditations, I want to deal more with changes we may make or projects we may take on. Having criticized our sexual attitudes or our policy on nuclear arms or our assumptions in foreign policy, what are we ordinary citizens to do? What I shall have to say will not be very original or very conclusive, but perhaps it will encourage others to follow through more effectively.

First, I think that citizens disturbed by the drift of their culture ought to sit back and think through how they themselves can best apply pressure to change it. Certainly the example they can give at home and at work is no small contribution. Indeed, if enough people say no to the materialism or militarism that seems to be shaping so much of the big picture, that picture finally will start to change. But it might also help to focus specifically on the votes that we have as members of a democracy, on the money that we spend as consumers and investors, and on the options we have about how we will spend our allegiance.

It is hard to make a case that the citizenry of the United States is Christian in the areas of sex, war, and international justice when it overwhelmingly votes for politicians whose express policies collide dramatically with the gospel. For all the signs I see that these people overall abhor the nuclear weapons that we keep producing, I am brought up short by their votes in national elections. In fact, the results of recent national elections amount to a sober counsel not to underestimate the credulity and fear and religious malformation of the citizenry at large. When farmers have voted again for leaders who have wantonly neglected them through the past four years, and businesspeople have voted again for leaders who have done virtually nothing to control the spiraling budget deficits, and women have voted in large numbers for leaders who have refused to support constitutional amendments on behalf of women's equality, one has to conclude that the populace as a whole is seriously underdeveloped. What is one to make of the large numbers of Christians who do not even seem to recognize the implications of their own rightful claims to fair treatment? Only a political activism based on an almost mystical faith that God will find a way to enlighten the blind is likely to allow one to keep moving forward.

We ourselves can vote our consciences, of course, and we can continue to work to try to enlighten them. We can and should express our views to other citizens in the unpretentious give and take that many situations at work or in church allow. In the measure that we feel skilled or inclined, we can work for politicians who seem to embody better views about peace and justice, and we can even consider running for office ourselves. As long as we calculate before we start to build such a tower, we can consider political service a genuine ministry.

Our money is also a factor worth trying to estimate, especially if we have sizable resources. We can check what we are buying and whether or not our lifestyle contradicts the materialism and consumerism of the culture at large the way that evangelical values would suggest. If we are not becoming leaner, sparer, and simpler, we probably are not deepening our hold on biblical poverty. If our money is going to help fan the national debt or prop up the war industries, it is at least a tendril of many evils. To be sure, the United States' economy is so complicated that it becomes a major research project to find our just where one's mutual funds or stocks are exerting pressure. It might be better for us, therefore, to put the money that is left when we calculate what we need to live simply but well into "stocks" that will pile up treasure in heaven: programs to help the poor, private little charities, church offices working for peace and justice, activities that protest war and advertise peace.

I realize very well that a great many people, perhaps the majority, have very little left over after they calculate what they themselves need to live simply and well. The costs of higher education alone are staggering. What I don't understand is how slow many such people are to realize that they are suffering such financial pressures largely because they live in a country that insists on massive preparations for (an impossible) war. Instead of wasting billions on weapons and useless luxuries, a sane U.S. economy would first of all be targeting the survival needs of the poor and the critical needs of all people's spirituality: education, basic scientific research, artistic beauty, leisure in which to think, reverence, pray, and exercise compassion.

Right now our money too often controls us, rather than vice versa. Right now we elect politicians who appeal to our baser instincts rather than politicians who stand for ideals compatible with the Christian gospel. We are taken in by avuncular speech and an image of "a nice guy," when, if we had any sense, we would be electing brains and competence. We prefer the worsening status quo to firm speech about the changes we must make if we expect to hold world leadership in the year 2020. It is hard to believe that people can be so gullible. It is depressing indeed to see millions led astray by red herrings and rhetorical ploys. Humorists like Art Buchwald and Calvin Trillin but speak the truth when they say that the stuff coming out of Washington is much more bizarre than anything they could think up. But critical intelligence is snoozing and irony has gone on holiday, so the readership at large thinks that the Buchwalds and Trillins fall into the category of entertainers. Christian counterculturalism therefore often looms as a simple retrieval of a basic appreciation of satire.

For the satiric imagination, the door is open and one is starting to vote with one's feet. Radical criticism of one's culture or one's church brings the chill of solitude, the specter of cold nights in the desert. I do not think this need mean giving up one's love of country or church. The ache one feels says that love continues, because otherwise there would only be disgust. But the ache is potent, and it remains even when one has said the ritualistic sayings, and returned to the genuine truths, about human weakness and one's own large share in it. As too many Christians don't know, hope is not the same as optimism. Optimism is the groundless confidence of Pollyanna, standing there lumpishly with her smile button and her Mary Janes. Hope is the turn toward the spirit of Christ that comes in the wake of the crucifixion and resurrection. Jesus was full of such hope, because Jesus riveted all of his energies, those that we would call religious and those that we would call political, onto God in heaven. Jesus was not optimistic about human beings, because he had had a good schooling in the human heart.

There is much good in that heart, of course, but also much fear and twistedness. There is a central call to the light, but also a great will not to know. The unfortunate result is that a great many people only come to wisdom through suffering, and along the way they contribute to the sufferings of many others. A great many of us want the wrong things and keep ourselves stupid in order to justify this wanting. Therefore, Christians who hear the voice of God and do not harden their hearts emerge from their prayer quite radicalized. They know in their bones, all the while that they dread it, that the way of Christ leads to the cross of counterculturalism. If we will follow Christ, we will be strangers to all mammon, that which dominates our own fifty states and that which many other countries are revolting to try to attain. If we are strangers to mammon, our votes and the way we use our money and the place where our heart has come to lodge will show us fruits that many of our neighbors will call un-American. At that point, our love may start to become mature, for we will have to keep trying to feel affection for people who consider us their enemies, keep trying to do good to those who would like to persecute us.

What U.S. policies are compatible with the gospel? What U.S. policies are not?

Why do the majority of U.S. citizens vote for leaders who mainly put themselves forward as servants of material prosperity?

What is a proper sort of counterculturalism and prophetic radicalism?

29

The Gospel according to Wall Street

Read Luke 18:18-30

The solar plexus of the enemies of peace and justice, as I
see it, is the fixation that our culture has with money. As St.
Ignatius of Loyola put it in his *Spiritual Exercises,* the
Satanic way is to lead people from a love of money to a love
of honors and then finally to a pride or love of self that sets
them in revolt against God. Long before Loyola, Augustine
had intuited much the same thing, speaking of the love of self
that is a contempt of God as the characteristic feature of the
secular city. Probably not many people in our society are
such strong personalities that one may speak of any profound
"revolt" against God. In the main, beguilement with money
and distraction with pleasures or honors keep the majority of
sinners in their unease. But the chain between money, vain-
glory, and pride is sufficiently strong to merit our sober study.
If we can break this chain at the outset, by clashing head-on
with the values proposed to us by Wall Street and Madison
Avenue, we will have struck a big blow for peace and justice.

Consider, for example, the place of profits in the war
industry. Numerous firms make huge sums of money by
supplying our country and many others with grossly destructive weaponry. They tend to do this under the rationalization
that someone will satisfy the world's will to possess savage
arms so it might as well be themselves. As many managers of
such companies see it, their job is to maximize profits. If
weapons be the way to accomplish this, they will produce
weapons with a smile. Analogously, many people who man-

151

age companies or put together mergers and takeovers follow the profit motive. That is the gospel of U.S. business (of international business) as they see it. The idea that workers and towns have a stake in mergers, closures, moves, and the rest only occurs later on. The first time on the agenda, directing the entire agenda, is the profit motive.

The blunt fact is that this view of work and business cannot be squared with the gospel. Even if one argues that efficiency can be a religious virtue and that free enterprise is sponsored by the Book of Proverbs, the Sermon on the Mount and the Epistle of James and the classical Hebrew prophets rise up to say no. When people matter less than profits, work and business have become perverse. When the wants of the few wealthy weigh more than the needs of the many poor, an economy has its intentions in the wrong place. The basic features of a healthy economy are not difficult to summon. All people have the right to a living, a fair share of the goods of the earth. No people have the right to luxuries while other human beings lack necessities. One may play these evangelical tunes for the domestic economy or one may extend them to the worldwide interchange. The music will remain the same. I feel certain that as long as one is listening to the spirit of Christ, the tunes of most capitalists will sound discordant.

The good news preached by Wall Street, when subjected to but the briefest of analyses, turns out to be very thin gruel indeed. There is the consideration of how many can get in on it and the discouraging facts about worldwide poverty. There is the consideration of how much stuff a person can profitably use and the view of the traditional sages that for the spirit to wax fat the body had best grow lean. And, worst of all, there is the message and example of Christ, who himself had no place to lay his head. In this last context, the mansions of the wealthy look ludicrous, all the worse if the insignia inside proclaim them to be bishops or churchgoers.

The fact is that the heroes of humanity and religion became what they are with little regard for money. In some cases they grew up in fortunate circumstances, as the legends have it regarding the Buddha and history suggests about the Mahatma Gandhi. In other cases, such as that of Jesus and

Muhammad, the child learned from the beginning that the world was tilt and only God could set it straight. Either way, all of the gurus who have come to stand out in the annals of human wisdom have lived apart from a desire for money. All have seen that money is among the chief of the temptations that would tie them to the world and the self. Where God or ultimate reality was calling them to absorption in the deepest mysteries, money would have had them waste time on superficialia. Where their fellow human beings were raising up sores and dreadful depressions for them to heal, money would have reduced their medication to things. So they looked upon the Wall-Streeters of their day as Jesus looked upon the rich young man of Luke 18. The young man grew sad, for he had many possessions and the call of the Master demanded that he leave them. He could not, for he had learned too well the lessons of the Wall Street of his day and so feared to stand alone as a religious self rather than as a successful investor.

In television ads, Madison Avenue tells many serious investors that there are various companies with whom to sit down and hammer out a philosophy of making money. The target audience for the ads are solemn types indeed, burdened with the cares of making the world go round. Only their wheeling and dealing, their ads imply, continue to keep chaos at bay. The first part of a serious resistance to this pernicious packaging of mammon might well be to laugh in its face.

The second part could certainly be the traditional tactic of continuing to raise further questions. For example, what will the successful investor do once the targeted sums have been reached and the cool million lies in the vault earning gorgeous sums of tax-free interest? What will the leisure or pleasure that such financial security can allow go for? Will it be enough to have on the gravestone, "He made a wonderful pile"? If death were to come this day, what would he or she wish to have done? Jesus himself used this tactic, of course, calling the man who only thought of building bigger barns a thorough and self-destructive fool. The story of the poor man Lazarus and the rich man burning in hell is a not very subtle further question.

Through history other great spiritual masters, such as

Francis de Sales, updated this tactic of raising further questions. It may be harder in our own day, when we cannot assume that "heaven" and "hell" are potent symbols, but even diluted into the modern categories of genuine "success" and "failure," the gospel queries can continue to bite and prod. What *does* it profit a rich person to gain the whole world and end up with a corroded soul? How *can* one claim to love God or be a decent member of the species while one's heart is closed to the poor? Wall Street has no satisfying response to these questions and would prefer that they never be raised. But we have no fealty to Wall Street, unless we choose to hand over our birthright, so we should keep raising them, on and on and on.

Such a process of questioning, of course, takes us into the incomprehensible mystery of God. That is why wise Christian educators encourage it, and why Christianity has nothing to fear from either fully critical intelligence or genuine mysticism. Both bring home the primordial truth that God is the beginning, the end, the foundation, and the crux of all meaning.

For our contemplation of money, success, material possessions, and the other creatures whose abuse generates mammon, such a process of questioning can bring a most helpful delimitation or framing. Set in the frame of God's goodness, the brevity of human life, and the imperatives of loving God and our neighbor, our money, success, and material possessions all become means rather than ends. They are as helpful as the degree to which we use them to praise God and comfort suffering human beings. They are as harmful as the degree to which they keep us from these tasks. Zacchaeus can serve as a good model in this matter. Although he was immersed in money night and day, he made it serve his helpfulness toward the poor and he competely subordinated it to his thirst for the kingdom of God. Although Zacchaeus was a prominent maven on the Wall Street of his day, Jesus was able to bless his household with salvation.

What does the parable of Lazarus and the rich man condemned to hell suggest about the abvertising our children

*must take in if they are to watch Wimbledon or the U.S.
Open?*

*Describe a properly Christian satire of our culture's ab-
sorption with money.*

*How does the technique of continuing to raise further
questions show that the human person can only rest in God?*

30

Living by Matthew 25

Read Matthew 25:31-46

The last part of Matthew 25, verses 31-46, stands high in works by liberation theologians, for these verses offer perhaps the best summary of the paramount importance that Jesus attached to practical love of one's neighbor. Like all the individual portions of the New Testament, this pericope has to be interpreted in light of the evangelical whole. Yet even when one has added checks and balances from other places, the text rings with a disturbing clarity. For those who want a clear call to action, one couldn't conclude a book on peace and justice more appropriately than by pondering the implications and applications of Matthew 25.

The scene, which is of a judgment at the Parousia, is familiar. The Son of man, functioning as a king who has ascended his throne to administer a final justice, separates the sheep from the goats. And what is the basis for this separation? Those who are sheep or people who have found favor have acted positively on behalf of their neighbors. They have ministered to hunger, thirst, loneliness, nakedness, sickness, and imprisonment as they happened upon these in the course of their daily lives. More profoundly, the king who is Christ says that in ministering to people in these sorts of distress, the blessed of God who are to inherit the kingdom, have in fact ministered to himself. The "I" that rings throughout the passage is Matthew's equivalent of the Pauline "Body of Christ." The goats or rejected ones are cast out of the kingdom simply because they did not do these acts of kindness and helpfulness to their unprepossessing neighbors and so failed to succor Christ. Christians have seldom failed throughout history to appreciate the enormous implications in this scenario. Again and again, people who have spent their lives in nursing or relief of the poor or prison ministries have been motivated and consoled by the belief that they were serving Christ.

Recently I opened the pages of a religious newspaper and was saddened to read of the death of George MacRae, a Jesuit biblical scholar who had been Stillman Professor and Acting Dean at Harvard Divinity School. I had known George slightly since my student days and had been with him the previous summer in Boston. The reflective remarks that the author offered struck me quite forcibly. For George MacRae, the author said, one best found the love of God in the midst of ordinary people. When asked for a rationale for his energetic life of teaching, preaching, writing, and administration, George MacRae had simply pointed to the needy people who matched the ministerial talents that God had given him.

There are many forms of neediness, of course, and we are right to think that we might easily expand the list given in Matthew 25. I think we are also right, however, to sense that we should not wander too far from the specificity and physicality of the list that Matthew attributes to Jesus. When people are hungry and naked, we should not get sidetracked in overly reflective broodings about life in the ghetto or the sociology of modern poverty. We should first try to help them get something to eat and something to wear. That is the justice in the contention of conservative social analysts that direct, one-to-one forms of charity and relief will never go out of style. That is the form that many admirable works of charity, such as those of Mother Teresa of Calcutta, continue to assume. Yet the perhaps more removed matter of patterns and systems also deserves a place in the discussion. For while the one-to-one ministries to people in their specific here and now needs will always be necessary and admirable, we also need to put our shoulder to the wheels that might diminish the great number of such individual cases by improving our society's general patterns of employment, job-training, health insurance, education, and the like. There is plenty of work to go around, and we do not all have the same talents or inclinations. What we do all have, if we all are people trying to hear the scriptural word of God, is an obligation to treat our needy neighbors as we would want to treat Christ himself.

Traditional Christianity put some of this sense of obligation in the Latin tag, "Hospes venit, Christus venit: When a guest comes, Christ comes." Thus, most monastic rules enjoined hospitality, and ancient codes that forbade injuring any guest took on the sheen of Christian anointing. The house of God became a sanctuary for people fleeing vengeance, offering today's Christians a model for their work with draft resisters and illegal aliens. To meet a person in need, we might say by way of generalization, has traditionally been thought of as meeting the divine in the form it has chosen for its "regular" revelations. On the whole, the Christian God does not choose to be revealed through prodigies but through ordinary human interactions. If we fail to see this in the Hebrew Bible, where the authors teach it again and again, we certainly must see it in the Incarnation. Thus, the Johannine Christ can say that when we see him we see the Father, while Paul can identify the church whom he was persecuting with Jesus the risen Lord.

Many people who feel they have few gifts for prayer, reflection, solitude, and interiority have taken this message to heart. Thinking of themselves as doers rather than musers, they have sponsored all sorts of good works in their communities. From food banks to regular visits to the sick and the aged, they have honored the theology of Matthew 25. Without doubt they have both greatly improved their local communities and heaped up for themselves a rich heavenly reward.

The scale of human neediness around the world has now become such, however, that we need to take this Christian practicality to another plane. The most practical thing we can do, if we want to help alleviate the hunger and nakedness that afflict perhaps the majority of the world's population, is to press for changes in the current ways that the nations do business and prepare for war. The problem of world poverty does not boil down to a lack of natural resources. Nature continues to offer resources sufficient to provide a decent life

for a controlled human population. The problem of world
poverty results from the blinders that keep us from acknowl-
edging the cohumanity of all other peoples. If we took
seriously Jesus' imagery, which we should note makes no
mention of racial or sexual or religious limitations, we would
have to think of people in East Africa as suffering members
of our Lord. Perhaps that would help us make haste to get
them food and medical supplies. Perhaps it would also help
us want to change the current international economy and see
the blasphemy in our preparing to kill millions of our fellow
human beings.

Any confrontation like this between the depths of the
Christian sense of human solidarity and the nations' ways of
viewing one another shows the gigantic chasm separating
biblical revelation from secular pragmatism. Matthew 25
stands so far outside the horizon of the typical world politician or macroeconomist that for all practical purposes it
might never have been written. The typical world politician
knows little besides naked power and dollars or marks or
rubles or yen. The typical macroeconomist assumes that
people are bound to be competitive. Matthew 25 undercuts
all these assumptions, as the Bible so regularly does, by
focusing on direct actions. By doing the deeds that compassion summons, the biblical heroes reveal a completely super-
natural sense of God and their fellow human beings. To their
mind, we could cooperate as easily as we now compete, were
we to stand in God's light and grace. We could build bridges
of peace as easily as we raise up engines of war.

It is true that the New Testament more clearly depicts such
actions as the stuff of which ordinary human life might be
made than does the rather militant Old Testament, but the
New Testament thinks of Christ as the fulfillment of the
messianic prophecies, and the messianic prophecies are hardly less idealistic than the judgment scene of Matthew 25.
Indeed, for a prophet such as Isaiah, justice and peace will be
the hallmark of the reign of God's anointed one. He will be
wonderful, a counselor, a mighty God, the everlasting Father,
the prince of peace. Matthew 25 assumes that he has come
and that he is soon to come again. Matthew 25 implies that
each time we offer a cup of cold water in his name we both

save ourselves and give flesh to the nearly last words of
Revelation: "Come, Lord Jesus!" If we live by Matthew 25,
then, we need not worry that we are not doing our bit for
peace and justice. If we live by Matthew 25, we shall have a
chance to serve the prince of peace every day.

------

*How does the judgment scene in Matthew 25 cut short all
useless discussion of who is our neighbor?*

*How is Christ present in people we consider entirely
ordinary?*

*Does Matthew 25 vindicate interpreting the gospel as a
theology of liberation?*

Annotated Bibliography

American Friends Service Committee. *A Compassionate Peace*. New York: Hill and Wang, 1982. A competent and realistic analysis of how peace might come to the Middle East.

Brill, Earl H. *The Christian Moral Vision*. New York: Seabury, 1979. A good introductory volume on Christian ethics or moral theology.

Brown, Robert McAfee. *Making Peace in the Global Village*. Philadelphia: Westminster, 1981. Readable yet stimulating and challenging thoughts on Christian peacemaking.

————. *Unexpected News: Reading the Bible with Third World Eyes*. Philadelphia: Westminster, 1984. Liberation theology at its most biblical and personally challenging.

Carmody, Denise L. *The Double Cross*. New York: Crossroad, 1986. Christian feminist reflections on women's ordination and abortion.

————. *Seizing the Apple*. New York: Crossroad, 1984. The theory and practice of a centrist Christian feminist spirituality.

Carmody, John. *Ecology and Religion*. Ramsey, NJ: Paulist, 1983. A brief overview of the new theology that the ecological crisis seems to demand.

————. *Maturing a Christian Conscience*. Nashville: The Upper Room, 1985. Christian ethics as personal spirituality.

Crahan, Margaret E., ed. *Human Rights and Basic Needs in the Americas*. Washington, DC: Georgetown University Press, 1982. Christian orientations on the economic and political problems of Latin America.

Evans, Robert A. and Evans, Alice Frazer. *Human Rights*. Maryknoll, NY: Orbis, 1983. Case studies from around the world that spotlight the global interconnections of problems of justice and peace.

Fenton, Thomas P. *Education for Justice*. New York: Maryknoll, 1975. A somewhat dated but still provocative resource manual.

Gilligan, Carol. *In a Different Voice*. Cambridge, MA: Harvard University Press, 1982. A stimulating view of women's processes of maturation and decision making.

Gordon, Mary. *Men and Angels*. New York: Random House, 1985. A wonderfully intelligent novel that beautifully depicts the tensions of marriage and parenting nowadays.

Gremillion, Joseph, ed. *The Gospel of Peace and Justice*. Maryknoll, NY: Orbis, 1976. Papal documents on peace and justice prior to John Paul II.

Gremillion, Joseph and Ryan, William, eds. *World Faiths and the New World Order*. Washington, DC: The Interreligious Peace Colloquium, 1978. Essays by Christians, Muslims, and Jews on international problems of peace and justice.

Haughey, John C., ed. *Personal Values in Public Policy*. New York: Paulist, 1979. Studies by moral theologians that focus on how to import Christian values into the pluralistic realm of public policy making.

Hoban, Russell. *Riddley Walker*. New York: Washington Square, 1980. A magnificent novel depicting human life as it might be after nuclear holocaust.

Illich, Ivan. *Toward a History of Needs*. New York: Bantam, 1980. Essays by a maverick Christian educator who is steeped in a third-world perspective.

Joranson, Philip N. and Butigan, Ken, eds. *Cry of the Environment*. Santa Fe: Bear & Co., 1984. Essays by leading Christian ecologists that mainly argue for greater emphasis on the Christian doctrine of creation.

Kegan, Robert. *The Evolving Self*. Cambridge, MA: Harvard University Press, 1982. A persuasive study of human maturation that gives both independence and interrelation their due.

Kwitny, Jonathan. *Endless Enemies*. New York: Congdon & Weed, 1984. A critical reading of recent American foreign policy that concludes it has been badly misguided.

McGinnis, Kathleen and McGinnis, James. *Parenting for Peace and Justice*. Maryknoll, NY: Orbis, 1981. Helps for parents who want to make a Christian orientation toward peace and justice a family affair.

Merton, Thomas. *Conjectures of a Guilty Bystander*. New York: Doubleday, 1968. Profitable soul-searching by the Trappist monk

who posthumously has become one of the gurus of current ecumenical spirituality.

Naipaul, V. S. *Among the Believers*. New York: Vintage, 1982.
Disturbing impressions of a visit to Iran, Pakistan, Malaysia, and
Indonesia.

————. *India: A Wounded Civilization*. New York: Vintage,
1978. A critical look at the subcontinent through the eyes of a
Westernized Indian novelist and journalist.

Paton, Alan. *Ah, But Your Land is Beautiful*. New York: Charles
Scribner's Sons, 1982. A novel that, for Christian consciences, is
better than a dozen reports in *Time* magazine.

Santmire, H. Paul. *The Travail of Nature*. Philadelphia: Fortress,
1985. A largely historical study of the ambiguous place that nature
has held in Christian faith and theology.

Schillebeeckx, Edward. *God is New Each Moment*. New York:
Seabury, 1983. A wonderful blend of contemplative Christian faith
and a burning zeal for social justice.

Shinn, Roger L., ed. *Faith and Science in an Unjust World, Vol.
1*. Philadelphia: Fortress, 1980. The plenary session papers from
the World Council of Churches' conference at MIT in 1979 on this
summary theme.

Sider, Ronald J. and Brubaker, Darrel J., eds. *Preaching on
Peace*. Philadelphia: Fortress, 1982. Sermons by some of the
leading American Christian leaders of the opposition to the arms
race.

Simon, Arthur. *Bread for the World*. New York: Paulist, 1975. A
pioneering work on the worldwide spread of poverty and hunger.

Swidler, Arlene, ed. *Human Rights in Religious Traditions*. New
York: The Pilgrim Press, 1982. Essays originally published in *The
Journal of Ecumenical Studies* that offer the perspectives of the
different major world religious traditions.

Terkel, Studs. *American Dreams: Lost and Found*. New York:
Ballantine, 1980. Journalistic interviews with many different ordinary Americans that reveal the yearnings beneath many unpromising
exteriors.

Wren, Brian. *Education for Justice*. New York: Orbis, 1982.
Pedagogical principles for raising consciousness of the quiet imperative.

John Carmody is a Senior Research Fellow at the University of Tulsa in Oklahoma. He received a Ph.D. from Stamford University in California.

A theologian and a writer, Dr. Carmody has authored or co-authored twenty books, including *How to Make It Through the Day, Contemporary Catholic Theology, Maturing a Christian Conscience, Shamans, Prophets and Sages,* and *Becoming One Flesh,* which he co-wrote with his wife, Denise Lardner Carmody.